KT-116-826

everyday
easy
Cheap
eats

casseroles • stir-fries • savoury tarts • sweet treats

LONDON, NEW YORK, MELBOURNE,
MUNICH, AND DELHI

Designer
Elma Aquino

Editorial Assistant
Shashwati Tia Sarkar

Senior Jacket Creative
Nicola Powling

Managing Editor
Dawn Henderson, Angela Wilkes

Managing Art Editor
Christine Keilty

Production Editor
Maria Elia

Production Controller
Hema Gohil

Creative Technical Support
Sonia Charbonnier

DK INDIA

Head of Publishing
Aparna Sharma

Editors
Dipali Singh, Saloni Talwar

Designer
Devika Dwarkadas

DTP Co-ordinator
Sunil Sharma

DTP Designer
Tarun Sharma

Material first published in *The Cooking Book*, 2008
and *Cook Express*, 2009
This edition first published in Great Britain in 2010
by Dorling Kindersley Limited
80 Strand, London WC2R 0RL

A Penguin Company

2 4 6 8 10 9 7 5 3 1

A CIP catalogue record for this book
is available from the British Library.

ISBN 978-1-4053-5516-2

Colour reproduction by MDP, Bath
Printed and bound in Singapore by Star Standard

Discover more at
www.dk.com

CONTENTS

Being economical in the kitchen doesn't mean that you or your family need to go without good food. On the contrary, everyday recipes should be delicious and satisfying but not leave you out of pocket. This practicality is not new: in every part of the world, the most beloved traditional foods, such as Russian Borscht, Hungarian Goulash, Mexican Quesadillas, and Italian Lasagne, are inexpensive to make for this very reason. Traditional recipes are therefore featured often in this book. These are dishes that you can reproduce reliably day after day, and they have an undeniable feel-good factor.

You can make your food go further by using the advice in the Useful Information section. Planning your meals is the smart way to be frugal – by **Using Leftovers** effectively you can make your Sunday roast dinner, for instance, last for days. Try the Quick Fish Pie or Pork and Spring Greens recipes for some tasty ideas. **Batching and Freezing** is another way to maximise your ingredients and minimise wastage. When cooking in large quantities, freeze a batch for later – this is an excellent solution for busy weeknights when you have little time to cook. Many recipes in this book are ideal for batch cooking: try the Sweetcorn Chowder or Provençal Lamb.

Following this is a range of **Recipe Choosers** that showcase recipes by themes such as Comfort, Healthy, and Vegetarian so you can easily find something that takes your fancy. For cooks in a hurry, the Quick recipes chooser is the first place to look for inspiration.

A selection of step-by-step **Techniques** at the beginning of relevant chapters will refine your core cookery skills. Some techniques will save you time in the kitchen and ensure you get the most from your ingredients, whether you are peeling garlic or coring apples. Other techniques will help you achieve perfect results from your recipe, for example when you need a flavourful stock or faultless pastry.

Recipes in the **Soups and Sandwiches** section are ideal for lunches, light snacks, or to start off a meal. Nothing is better than a warming soup on a cold day: Chorizo and Tomato Soup, Spiced Butternut Squash Soup, and Scotch Broth are all soul-soothing delights. Kids will love the classic sandwich Tuna Melt and spicy Mexican Tacos are the perfect weeknight family supper.

Big, hearty **Casseroles and Bakes** are slow-cooked to get sensational flavour from simple ingredients. They are wonderfully easy to make, too – prepare the ingredients, put them in a casserole or baking dish, then get on with something else (or put your feet up!) while your meal bubbles away in the oven or on the hob. Satisfying dishes such as Chicken with Cider and Cream and Sausage and Mustard Casserole are guaranteed crowd-pleasers.

When you're pushed for time, the **Stir-fries** section will give you plenty of ideas for quick meals. Whether you're looking for an elegant supper of Crispy Rice Noodles with Beef or the perfect breakfast of Parsi Eggs, stir-fries are affordable meals that are ultra-convenient. These one-pot wonders won't leave much washing up to be done either!

Fantastically versatile, great for any occasion, and much easier to make than you might think, **Pies and Tarts** are very rewarding to bake. In this section you'll find everything from exotic Empanadas to homely Sausage and Tomato Pie – eat hot or cold, indoors or outdoors.

After making all the savings on your shopping bill, you'll deserve something from the **Puddings** section. Old-fashioned family favourites such as Bread and Butter Pudding, Plum Crumble, and Baked Jam Roll are brilliant comfort foods that are kind to the wallet.

Home cooking is the best way to enjoy great food on a budget. Give all of these recipes a try and see just how easy it is to do every day.

Using leftovers

Cooking a dish one day and enjoying it in different ways in the days to come is a clever way to plan your weekly meals. Using leftover vegetables and meat in new and creative ways is not only thrifty, but also a great time-saver.

LEFTOVER	NEW DISH
VEGETABLES **Store** cooked root vegetables in a rigid airtight plastic container. Don't overpack, as they can go soggy. Leave to cool before sealing. Store greens in a covered bowl or rigid plastic container. Leave to cool before covering or sealing. **Refrigerate** cooked vegetables and greens for 1–2 days. **Freeze** leftover root vegetables that have been slightly undercooked. Keep for up to 1 month.	Root vegetables can be turned into bakes, pasta sauces, and frittatas. Leftover greens can be added to casseroles, lasagne, and soups. Alternatively, just reheat greens in a little olive oil, and toss in lemon juice and chilli oil. Serve with some fresh crusty bread.
POULTRY **Store** the meat and carcass separately, wrapped in cling film, then foil. Refrigerate within 2 hours after it has been cooked. Keep away from uncooked meats. Leftover stuffing and gravy should be stored separately in airtight containers. **Refrigerate** the meat and carcass for 2–3 days; use leftover gravy within 2 days. **Freeze** for up to 3 months. Defrost completely before use.	Chicken bones and meat can be used to prepare stock. Leftover poultry can be added to soups, warm salads, and noodle dishes. Or use it to make a pasta bake or a fragrant pilaf. Remember to reheat leftover poultry till it is piping hot.
MEAT **Store** beef, lamb, and pork away from uncooked meats. Refrigerate within 2 hours after it has been cooked. Leftover gravy can be stored in a plastic container. **Refrigerate** meat for 1–3 days; use leftover gravy within 2 days. **Freeze** for up to 3 months. Defrost completely before use.	Leftover meat can be added to casseroles, stir-fries, bakes, and pies. Alternatively, use it in casseroles and pasta bakes. Minced, it can be made into pies such as Shepherd's Pie. Remember to reheat leftover meat till it is piping hot.
FISH **Store** in a shallow rigid plastic container and seal, or put on a plate and wrap well with cling film. Store away from uncooked foods. Refrigerate within 2 hours after it has been cooked. **Refrigerate** for 1–2 days. **Freeze** for up to 3 months. Defrost completely before use.	Leftover fish can be added to salads, pastas, and pies. You can also use it to make fish cakes. Remember to reheat leftover fish till it is piping hot.

Batching and freezing

Make-ahead dishes for the freezer save you time and effort. To use them, thaw them slowly overnight in the refrigerator; it is not only the safest way to defrost, but also the best way to retain the food's flavour and texture.

FOOD	PACKAGING	STORAGE	DEFROST
SOUPS Once cooked, leave to cool completely, then pack into 500ml (16fl oz) portions. Don't freeze in over-large portions, as defrosting will take too long.	Pack in sealable freezer bags or plastic containers. Spoon stock into ice cube trays and freeze. Once frozen, remove from tray and transfer to a freezer bag and seal.	Soups for up to 3 months. Stocks for up to 6 months.	Thaw overnight in the refrigerator, then reheat in a pan until piping hot, or heat in the microwave on High for a few minutes.
STEWS Foods with a very high fat content will go rancid after a couple of months in the freezer, so choose lean cuts of meat. Cool completely before freezing.	Freeze in sealable freezer bags or foil containers, or ladle into rigid sealable plastic containers. Make sure meat is well covered with liquid, otherwise it will dry out.	Up to 3 months.	Thaw overnight in the refrigerator, then reheat in a pan, or in the oven at 180°C (350°F/Gas 4), for about 30 minutes, or until piping hot, or heat in the microwave on High for a few minutes.
PIES Baking is the ideal time to batch cook. You can freeze pastry cooked or uncooked. Cool completely before freezing.	**Uncooked:** Freeze blocks of pastry layered with wax paper, then wrapped in cling film. **Cooked:** Freeze pastry cases and pies wrapped in a double layer of cling film.	Uncooked pies and pastry for up to 3 months. Cooked pies and pastry cases for up to 6 months.	Bake uncooked pastries from frozen at 200°C (400°F/Gas 6), for 15 minutes. Thaw cooked pies overnight, then bake at 180°C (350°F/Gas 6) for 30 minutes, or until piping hot.

A guide to symbols

The recipes in this book are accompanied by symbols that alert you to important information.

Tells you how many people the recipe serves, or how much is produced.

Indicates how much time you will need to prepare and cook a dish. Next to this symbol you will also find out if additional time is required for such things as marinating, standing, or cooling. Read the recipe to find out exactly how much extra time to allow.

Points out a healthy dish – low in fat or has a low GI (Glycemic Index).

This is especially important, as it alerts you to what has to be done before you can begin to cook the recipe, or to parts of the recipe that may take a long time to complete.

This denotes that special equipment is required, such as a deep-fat fryer or skewers. Where possible, alternatives are given.

This symbol accompanies freezing information.

RECIPE CHOOSERS

Healthy

Chicken stir-fried with spring onion, basil, and lemongrass page 122

Spicy garlic green vegetable medley page 108

Aduki bean stew page 82

Smoked fish and anchovy gratin page 94

Ribollita page 64

Chicken with noodles and basil page 118

Pork and spring greens page 110

Baby courgettes with fish and couscous page 104

Spiced bean and herb hash page 102

Asian turkey and noodle soup page 50

Hungarian goulash page 78

Chickpea and vegetable stew page 90

Courgette, herb, and lemon tagine page 70

Quick – Savoury

Tuna melt page 42

Chickpeas with spinach page 120

Fried mozzarella sandwich page 34

Reuben sandwich page 60

Chorizo with peppers page 130

Quick fish pie page 86

Quesadillas with ham, gherkin, and smoked cheese page 62

Quick – Sweet

Bananas flambéed with Calvados page 204

Chocolate puddings page 194

Lemon and sugar crêpes page 212

Pear gratin page 206

Semolina page 200

Sticky toffee and banana pudding page 196

Kaiserschmarrn page 208

Vegetarian

Feta filo pie page 180

Chickpea and vegetable stew page 90

Sweetcorn chowder page 36

Fried mozzarella sandwich page 34

Gruyère tart page 160

Leek and cheese flamiche page 174

Cauliflower soup page 38

Aduki bean stew page 82

Chickpeas with spinach page 120

Parmesan cheese and walnut tart page 164

Spicy garlic green vegetable medley page 108

Vichyssoise page 44

Quesadillas with salsa Mexicana page 48

Spiced butternut squash soup page 46

Cheesy spinach pie page 154

Spiced bean and herb hash page 102

Light bites

Vegetable samosas page 146

Chorizo with peppers page 130

Pan bagnat page 52

Goat's cheese tartlets page 142

Quesasdillas with salsa Mexicana page 48

Feta and pumpkin pastries page 156

Croque monsieur page 57

Cheese and pepper jalousie page 176

Patatas bravas page 128

Empanadas page 150

Parsi eggs page 116

Sweetcorn and pepper filo triangles page 179

Comfort – Savoury

Tomato and chorizo soup page 40

Chicken with cider and cream page 80

Sweetcorn chowder page 36

Steak and ale pie page 168

Borscht page 32

Sausage and mustard casserole page 100

Pork and bean stew page 76

Chicken with pancetta, peas, and mint page 88

Steak and kidney pudding page 172

Comfort – Sweet

Sticky toffee and banana pudding page 196

Plum crumble page 202

Apple Charlotte page 188

Blueberry cobbler page 186

Rice pudding page 198

Baked jam roll page 214

SOUPS AND SANDWICHES

Make vegetable stock

Simmering water with vegetables will capture their delicate flavour. Use the stock to flavour vegetarian soups, stews, and risottos.

1 Place chopped carrots, celery, onions, and a bouquet garni into a large stockpot. Cover with water and bring to the boil. Reduce the heat and simmer the stock for up to 1 hour.

2 Ladle the stock through a fine sieve, pressing the vegetables against the sieve to extract any extra liquid. Season to taste with salt and pepper, let cool, and refrigerate for up to 3 days.

Make chicken stock

Use home-made chicken stock for soups, stews, and risottos.

1 Add raw chicken bones, or the bones and scraps from a cooked chicken into a large stockpot with carrots, celery, onions, and a bouquet garni. Cover with water and bring to the boil.

2 Reduce the heat and simmer for 2–3 hours, skimming frequently. Ladle the stock through a fine sieve and season to taste. Let cool and refrigerate for up to 3 days.

Make quesadillas

Quesadillas are essentially toasted sandwiches, using tortillas. You can use wheat or corn tortillas, and fill them with cheese and your favourite ingredients.

1 Have all your ingredients ready-prepared – 2 tortillas, and your chosen fillings. Here we're using 25g (scant 1oz) Gruyère cheese, grated, and a handful of sliced jalapeño chillies from a jar.

2 Heat a frying pan with a little olive oil (you can omit this if you prefer), then place one tortilla in the pan. Add the topping ingredients, leaving a little room around the edge so the cheese doesn't spill out.

3 Lay the other tortilla precisely over the top and press down firmly with a spatula to seal, paying particular attention to the edges. Leave it to warm through for a couple of minutes.

4 Flip the quesadilla over and leave it to cook on the other side for a minute or two. When cooked through, transfer to a plate, and slice into halves or quarters. Serve immediately while hot.

Salmorejo

A fresh soup from southern Spain, this is similar to gazpacho, the popular chilled Spanish soup.

INGREDIENTS

115g (4oz) stale white bread, crusts removed, torn into bite-sized pieces
3 tbsp olive oil, plus extra to serve
2 tbsp red wine vinegar
1 onion, roughly chopped
3 garlic cloves
1 red pepper, deseeded and chopped
5 tomatoes, skinned and deseeded
1 cucumber, peeled, deseeded, and chopped
salt and freshly ground black pepper
2 hard-boiled eggs, chopped
2 slices of serrano ham, cut into strips

METHOD

1 Place the bread into a bowl. Add the oil and vinegar, mix well, and set aside to soak for 10 minutes.

2 Place the onion, garlic, red pepper, tomatoes, and most of the cucumber in a blender or food processor with 90ml (3fl oz) water, and blend to a purée. Add the bread mixture, blend again, then season to taste with salt and pepper.

3 Chill for at least 30 minutes, pour into serving bowls, and top with the hard-boiled eggs, strips of ham, and the remaining cucumber. Serve, drizzled with a little olive oil.

serves 4

prep 15 mins, plus soaking and chilling

blender or food processor

Sopa de tortilla

Fresh lime juice, coriander, and dried poblano chillies give a Mexican flavour to this tomato soup.

serves 4

prep 15 mins • cook 50 mins

food processor or blender

INGREDIENTS

5 tbsp sunflower oil
$\frac{1}{2}$ onion, finely chopped
2 large garlic cloves, finely chopped
450g (1lb) tomatoes, skinned
1.5 litres ($2\frac{3}{4}$ pints) chicken stock or vegetable stock
1 or 2 dried poblano chillies, deseeded
2 soft corn tortillas, cut into strips
3 tbsp chopped coriander
2 tbsp fresh lime juice
salt and freshly ground black pepper
85g (3oz) Gruyère cheese, grated
2 limes, cut into wedges, to serve

METHOD

1 Heat 1 tablespoon of the oil in a large saucepan over a medium heat. Add the onion and fry, stirring, for 5 minutes, or until softened. Add the garlic and stir for 30 seconds. Transfer to a food processor or blender with the tomatoes and process until smooth.

2 Tip the purée into the pan and simmer for 8–10 minutes, stirring constantly. Stir in the stock and bring to the boil. Reduce the heat, partially cover the pan, and simmer for 15 minutes, or until the soup has thickened.

3 Place a non-stick frying pan over a medium heat. Add the chillies and press them flat against the pan with a spatula until they blister, then repeat for the other side. Remove from the pan, cut into small pieces, and set aside.

4 Heat the remaining oil in the frying pan until sizzling hot. Add the tortilla strips in batches and fry just until crisp. Remove with a slotted spoon and drain on kitchen paper.

5 When ready to serve, add the chillies to the soup, bring to the boil and simmer for 3 minutes, or until the chillies are soft. Stir in the coriander, lime juice, and salt and pepper to taste. Ladle the soup into 4 bowls. Divide the toasted tortilla strips between the bowls, top with a sprinkling of cheese, and serve with lime wedges.

PREPARE AHEAD Steps 1–4 can be prepared up to 1 day in advance and the tortilla strips stored in an airtight container.

Tacos

Taco shells can be filled with all sorts of spicy fillings and make great party food.

INGREDIENTS

2 tbsp sunflower oil
500g (1lb 2oz) lean minced beef
2–3 tbsp taco seasoning
12 taco shells
lettuce, shredded, to serve
Cheddar cheese, grated, to serve

METHOD

1 Heat the oil in a large frying pan and cook the minced beef until evenly browned, stirring occasionally. Add the taco seasoning and stir in 120ml (4fl oz) water. Simmer over a low heat for 10 minutes, or until the meat mixture is thickened.

2 Just before the meat is ready, warm the taco shells in a low oven for 3–4 minutes.

3 Spoon the meat into the shells and top each with shredded lettuce and Cheddar cheese.

GOOD WITH Tomato salsa, jalapeño peppers, and soured cream.

Borscht

This classic Russian soup is thickly textured and satisfying.

INGREDIENTS

2 large beetroot
1 onion
1 carrot
1 celery stick
45g (1½oz) butter or goose fat
400g can chopped tomatoes
1 garlic clove, crushed (optional)
1.7 litres (3 pints) vegetable stock
2 bay leaves
4 cloves
2 tbsp lemon juice
salt and freshly ground black pepper

METHOD

1 Roughly grate the beetroot, onion, carrot, and celery stick.

2 Melt the butter in a large saucepan over a medium heat. Add the vegetables and cook, stirring, for 5 minutes, or until just softened.

3 Add the tomatoes and crushed garlic, if using, and cook for 2–3 minutes, stirring frequently, then stir in the stock.

4 Tie the bay leaves and cloves in a small piece of muslin and add to the pan. Bring the soup to the boil, then reduce the heat, cover, and simmer for 1 hour 20 minutes.

5 Discard the muslin bag. Stir in the lemon juice and season to taste with salt and pepper. Ladle the soup into warm bowls, and serve.

GOOD WITH A garnish of soured cream or grated carrot, and chunks of dark rye bread.

serves 4

prep 15 mins • cook 1 hr 30 mins

muslin

Fried mozzarella sandwich

Served hot, this truly indulgent snack has a melting centre.

INGREDIENTS

8 slices of sourdough bread
olive oil
150g (5½oz) mozzarella, sliced
12 mi-cuit tomatoes (roasted, semi-dried), roughly chopped
2 handfuls of basil, torn
salt and freshly ground black pepper

METHOD

1 Lay the slices of bread on a board and drizzle both sides lightly with olive oil.

2 Top 4 of the slices of bread with the mozzarella, tomatoes, and torn basil, and season to taste with salt and pepper.

3 Top with the remaining bread slices and squash down with your hands, making sure none of the filling is sticking out.

4 Heat a large frying pan and add 1 tablespoon of olive oil. Carefully add 2 of the sandwiches and fry for 2–3 minutes, on each side, or until golden. Set aside and keep warm while frying the other 2 sandwiches.

5 Slice each sandwich in half and serve.

GOOD WITH Wild rocket leaves drizzled with balsamic vinegar.

serves 4

prep 10 mins
• cook 12 mins

Sweetcorn chowder

Full of potatoes and sweetcorn, this is a simple but tasty, chunky soup.

INGREDIENTS

2 tbsp olive oil
2 onions, finely chopped
salt and freshly ground black pepper
6–8 medium potatoes, peeled and cut into bite-sized pieces
2 x 340g cans sweetcorn, drained
1.4 litres (2½ pints) hot vegetable stock
handful of flat-leaf parsley, finely chopped
4 tbsp double cream (optional), to serve

METHOD

1 Heat the oil in a large pan, add the onions, and cook over a low heat for 6–8 minutes, or until soft and translucent. Season well with salt and pepper, then stir in the potatoes and cook over a low heat for 5 minutes.

2 Mash the sweetcorn a little with the back of a fork, then add to the pan. Pour in the stock, bring to the boil, then reduce to a simmer and cook for 15 minutes, or until the potatoes are soft. Stir through the parsley and season again with salt and pepper if needed.

3 Stir through the cream (if using), ladle into bowls, and serve.

PREPARE AHEAD This recipe makes a large quantity so you may want to freeze some. Before adding the cream, let cool completely, transfer to a freezerproof container, then freeze. To serve, defrost in the refrigerator overnight, then reheat in a pan until piping hot. Stir through the cream (if using), and serve.

serves 8

prep 15 mins
• cook 25 mins

healthy option (without the cream)

freeze for up to 3 months

Cauliflower soup

The potatoes and cauliflower give this soup a silky texture.

serves 8

prep 15 mins • cook 40 mins

healthy option (without the cream)

blender or food processor

INGREDIENTS

2 tbsp olive oil
2 onions, finely chopped
salt and freshly ground black pepper
3 garlic cloves, grated or finely chopped
4 celery sticks, finely chopped
2 bay leaves
675g (1½lb) potatoes, peeled and cut into bite-sized pieces
1.4 litres (2½ pints) hot vegetable stock
2 cauliflowers, trimmed and cut into florets
drizzle of double cream, to serve (optional)

METHOD

1 Heat the oil in a large pan, add the onions, and cook over a low heat for 6–8 minutes, or until soft and translucent. Season well with salt and pepper, then add the garlic, celery, and bay leaves, and cook for 5 minutes, or until the celery begins to soften. Stir in the potatoes and cook for 5 minutes, then pour in the stock, bring to the boil, and cook for 15 minutes, or until the potatoes are nearly soft.

2 Add the cauliflower and cook for 10 minutes, or until it is soft but not watery. Remove the bay leaves and discard, then transfer the soup to a blender or food processor and process until smooth. Add a little more hot stock if it seems too thick. Taste, and season with salt and pepper if needed. Drizzle with double cream (if using), and serve.

GOOD WITH Warm crusty rolls and a sprinkling of ground cumin in each bowl to add a warming, spicy flavour.

Tomato and chorizo soup

Chickpeas add extra substance to the Spanish flavours of this soup.

INGREDIENTS

2 tbsp olive oil
250g (9oz) chorizo, cut into small cubes
2 red onions, finely chopped
4 celery sticks, finely diced
4 carrots, finely diced
3 garlic cloves, grated or finely chopped
salt and freshly ground black pepper
700g jar passata
1.2 litres (2 pints) hot vegetable stock
2 x 400g cans chickpeas, drained and rinsed
handful of coriander, finely chopped, to serve

METHOD

1 Heat half the oil in a large heavy-based pan, add the chorizo, and cook over a medium heat, stirring occasionally, for 5 minutes, or until beginning to turn crispy. Remove and put to one side.

2 Heat the remaining oil in the pan, add the onions, and cook over a low heat for 6–8 minutes, or until soft and translucent. Stir in the celery, carrots, and garlic, season with salt and pepper, then cook over a low heat, stirring occasionally, for 8 minutes, or until tender. Add the passata, stock, and chickpeas, and simmer for 15 minutes. Return the chorizo to the pan, then taste and season with salt and pepper if needed. Stir through the coriander and serve.

PREPARE AHEAD This recipe makes a large quantity so you may want to freeze some. Before adding the coriander, let cool completely, transfer to a freezeproof container, then freeze. To serve, defrost in the refrigerator overnight, then transfer to a pan and heat until piping hot. Stir in some chopped coriander, and serve.

serves 8

prep 20 mins
• cook 40 mins

freeze for up to 3 months

Tuna melt

This American diner classic really melts in the mouth.

INGREDIENTS

4 English muffins
1 tbsp olive oil
2 shallots, finely chopped
1 red pepper, deseeded and finely chopped
4 spring onions, thinly sliced
2 x 185g cans tuna chunks, drained
2 tbsp tomato ketchup or tomato relish
6 tbsp lemon mayonnaise
4 large, thin slices of mature Cheddar cheese or Edam cheese, halved diagonally

METHOD

1 Heat the grill to high. Split each muffin in half and toast the cut sides.

2 Heat the oil in a frying pan and gently fry the shallot, red pepper, and spring onions, stirring frequently, until softened but not browned. Add the tuna, breaking up the chunks with a fork. Cook for 1 minute, or until the tuna is heated through, then remove the pan from the heat and stir in the tomato ketchup or relish and 2 tbsp of the mayonnaise.

3 Spread the remaining mayonnaise over the cut sides of the muffins, spoon the tuna mixture on to 4 of the muffin halves, keeping the other 4 to top the sandwiches. Arrange the cheese triangles over the tuna.

4 Pop under the grill until the cheese melts and top with the muffin "lids". Serve at once.

GOOD WITH A selection of your favourite pickles such as pickled cucumbers and sweetcorn relish.

serves 4

prep 15 mins
• cook 10 mins

Vichyssoise

Despite its French name, this silky, smooth chilled soup originates from America.

INGREDIENTS

30g (1oz) butter
3 large leeks, green ends discarded, finely sliced
2 potatoes, about 175g (6oz) in total, peeled and chopped
1 celery stick, roughly chopped
1.2 litres (2 pints) vegetable stock
salt and freshly ground black pepper
150ml (5fl oz) double cream, plus extra to serve
2 tbsp finely chopped chives, to serve

METHOD

1 Heat the butter in a heavy saucepan over a medium heat and add the leeks. Press a piece of damp greaseproof paper on top, cover, and cook, shaking gently from time to time, for 15 minutes, or until the leeks are softened and golden.

2 Add the potatoes, celery, and stock, and season with salt and pepper. Bring to the boil, stirring, then cover and simmer for 30 minutes, or until the vegetables are tender.

3 Remove the pan from the heat and leave to cool slightly, then process in a blender until very smooth, in batches if necessary. Season to taste with salt and pepper and allow the soup to cool completely before stirring in the cream. Chill for at least 3 hours before serving.

4 To serve, pour into serving bowls, lightly stir in a little extra cream, and sprinkle with chives and pepper.

serves 4

prep 15 mins, plus chilling • cook 45 mins

chill for at least 3 hrs

blender

Spiced butternut squash soup

You could use any winter squash for this spicy, comforting soup.

INGREDIENTS

2 tbsp olive oil
2 onions, finely chopped
salt and freshly ground black pepper
3 garlic cloves, grated or finely chopped
4 sage leaves, finely chopped
2 red chillies, deseeded and finely chopped
pinch of freshly grated nutmeg
1 large butternut squash or 2 small ones, halved, peeled, deseeded, and chopped into small pieces
2 potatoes, peeled and diced
1.4 litres (2½ pints) hot vegetable stock
chilli oil, to serve
Gruyère cheese, grated, to serve

METHOD

1 Heat the oil in a large pan, add the onions, and cook over a low heat for 6–8 minutes, or until soft and translucent. Season with salt and pepper, then stir through the garlic, sage, chillies, and nutmeg, and cook for a few seconds.

2 Stir in the squash, add the potatoes and stock, and bring to the boil. Reduce to a simmer and cook for 20–30 minutes, or until the squash and potatoes are soft. Transfer to a blender or food processor and process until smooth. Taste, and season again with salt and pepper. Serve with a drizzle of chilli oil, and a sprinkling of Gruyère cheese.

serves 8

prep 20 mins • cook 40 mins

healthy option

blender or food processor

Quesadillas with salsa Mexicana

Traditionally, quesadillas are deep-fried. This method is a healthier option.

INGREDIENTS

8 flour tortillas
200g (7oz) mature Cheddar cheese, grated
guacamole, to serve

For the salsa Mexicana

2 tomatoes, finely chopped
½ onion, finely chopped
1 green chilli, deseeded and finely chopped
handful of coriander leaves, chopped
1 tsp salt
juice of ½ lime

METHOD

1 Heat a heavy frying pan over a medium heat. Make the salsa by combining all the ingredients in a bowl, then set aside.

2 Place 1 tortilla flat in the pan and heat for 30 seconds. Sprinkle 25g (scant 1oz) of the cheese over the surface. Top with another tortilla and press down lightly with a spatula.

3 Flip the quesadilla over, and cook until it is toasted on both sides and the cheese has melted. Repeat with the remaining tortillas.

4 Cut each quesadilla in halves or quarters, and serve immediately with the salsa Mexicana and guacamole on the side.

serves 4

prep 10 mins
• cook 20 mins

Asian turkey and noodle soup

A light, fragrant, and restorative broth.

INGREDIENTS

900ml ($1\frac{1}{2}$ pints) vegetable stock
2 tbsp soy sauce
1 stalk lemongrass, sliced
2.5cm (1in) piece of fresh root ginger, peeled and sliced
2 skinless turkey breast fillets, about 400g (14oz) each
300g (10oz) fine rice noodles
1 red chilli, deseeded and sliced
handful of coriander leaves
pinch of salt

METHOD

1 Heat the vegetable stock in a large saucepan over a medium heat. Once hot, add the soy sauce, lemongrass, ginger, and turkey breast fillets. Bring to the boil, reduce the heat slightly, and simmer for 15–20 minutes until the turkey is cooked through. Remove the turkey fillets with a slotted spoon and set aside to cool.

2 To cook the noodles, bring the poaching liquid to the boil, topping up with boiling water if needed. Add the rice noodles and chilli, reduce the heat slightly, and simmer for 1 minute. Shred the turkey and return it to the pan, with the coriander leaves, to heat through. Season with salt to taste, and serve immediately.

serves 4

prep 10 mins, plus cooling • cook 30 mins

healthy option

Pan bagnat

Popular in the area around Nice in the south of France, the name of this traditional worker's sandwich roughly translates as "wet bread".

INGREDIENTS

4 small, crusty loaves, such as half ciabattas or mini baguettes
2 garlic cloves, cut in half
2 tbsp olive oil
1 tsp white wine vinegar
salt and freshly ground black pepper
1 hard-boiled egg, sliced
2 large or 3 medium tomatoes, sliced
1/4 cucumber, sliced
12 anchovy fillets
100g can tuna, drained and flaked
1/2 green pepper, deseeded and sliced
2 spring onions, sliced
60g (2oz) cooked green beans
8 black olives, pitted and sliced
8 basil leaves

METHOD

1 Cut each loaf in half and scoop out most of the soft crumbs. Rub the insides of the loaves with the cut sides of the garlic cloves, drizzle with the olive oil and vinegar, and season to taste with salt and pepper.

2 Fill the loaves with the eggs, tomatoes, cucumber, anchovies, tuna, green pepper, spring onions, green beans, olives, and basil leaves, dividing the filling ingredients evenly between the loaves.

3 Wrap the loaves in cling film and chill in the refrigerator for at least 1 hour before serving.

serves 4
prep 20 mins, plus chilling

Scotch broth

A traditional, stew-like soup, this Scottish dish is extremely filling.

INGREDIENTS

450g (1lb) neck of lamb
salt and freshly ground black pepper
2 tbsp olive oil
1 onion, finely chopped
4 carrots, finely chopped
4 celery sticks, finely chopped
2.3 litres (4 pints) hot light chicken stockw
225g (8oz) pearl barley
handful of curly-leaf parsley, finely chopped

METHOD

1 Put the lamb in a large pan, cover with cold water, and season with salt and pepper. Bring to the boil, then lower the heat and simmer for 30 minutes, or until cooked. Remove with a slotted spoon, leave to cool slightly, then shred and put to one side. Reserve the cooking liquid.

2 Heat the oil in a large pan, add the onion, and cook over a low heat for 5 minutes, or until soft and translucent. Add the carrots and celery, and cook over a very low heat for 10 minutes. Strain the reserved liquid, then add to the pan, and pour in the stock. Season with salt and pepper, then add the pearl barley and lamb. Bring to the boil, then reduce to a simmer, and cook over a very low heat for 1 hour, or until the pearl barley is cooked. Top up with hot water if it begins to dry out too much. Stir through the parsley, then taste, and season again with salt and pepper if needed.

PREPARE AHEAD This recipe makes a large quantity so you may want to freeze some. Before adding the parsley, let cool completely, transfer to a freezeproof container, ensuring the lamb is completely covered in liquid, and freeze. To serve, defrost in the refrigerator overnight, then reheat in a pan until piping hot. Stir through the parsley, and serve.

serves 8

prep 20 mins • cook 1 hr 45 mins

freeze for up to 3 months

Croque monsieur

In France, these toasted cheese and ham sandwiches are a popular snack.

INGREDIENTS

400g (14oz) Gruyère cheese
60g (2oz) butter, plus extra for spreading
2 tbsp plain flour
2 tsp Dijon mustard
150ml (5fl oz) milk
8 slices of white sandwich bread
8 thin slices of ham

METHOD

1 Cut 115g (4oz) of the cheese into thin slices and grate the rest.

2 Melt the butter in a saucepan over a low heat. Remove from the heat and stir in the flour. Return to the hob and cook for 1 minute. Remove from the heat again and stir in the grated cheese, mustard, and milk. When smooth, set aside until ready to use.

3 Toast 4 of the bread slices on 1 side only. Spread the untoasted sides lightly with butter and top with the ham and cheese slices. Press the remaining 4 slices of bread on top and spread with the cheese mixture.

4 Grill until the cheese is bubbling and golden brown. Slice each one diagonally, and serve at once.

GOOD WITH A side salad and a portion of French fries for a quick but satisfying lunch.

PREPARE AHEAD Steps 1 and 2 can be completed 1 day in advance but the assembled croque monsieurs must be eaten immediately after toasting.

serves 4

prep 15 mins • cook 10 mins

White bean soup

This thick soup from northern Italy is guaranteed to keep out the winter chills.

serves 4

prep 30 mins, plus soaking • cook 2 hrs

before starting the recipe, soak the beans overnight

blender or hand mill

INGREDIENTS

3 tbsp olive oil
2 onions, finely chopped
2 garlic cloves, crushed
225g (8oz) dried cannellini beans, soaked overnight
1 celery stick, chopped
1 bay leaf
3 or 4 parsley stalks, without leaves
1 tbsp lemon juice
1.2 litres (2 pints) vegetable stock
salt and freshly ground black pepper
3 shallots, thinly sliced
60g (2oz) pancetta, chopped (optional)
85g (3oz) Fontina cheese or Taleggio cheese, chopped into small pieces

METHOD

1 Heat 2 tbsp of the olive oil in a saucepan, add the onions, and fry over a low heat for 10 minutes, or until softened, stirring occasionally. Add the garlic and cook, stirring, for 1 minute.

2 Drain the soaked beans and add to the pan with the celery, bay leaf, parsley stalks, lemon juice, and stock. Bring to the boil, cover, and simmer for 1½ hours, or until the beans are soft, stirring occasionally.

3 Remove the bay leaf and liquidize the soup in batches in a blender, or through a hand mill. Rinse out the pan. Return the soup to the pan and season to taste with salt and pepper.

4 Heat the remaining olive oil in a small frying pan, and fry the shallots and pancetta (if using), until golden and crisp, stirring frequently to stop them sticking to the pan.

5 Reheat the soup, adding a little stock or water if it is too thick. Stir the cheese into the soup. Ladle into individual bowls, and sprinkle each serving with the shallots and pancetta.

Reuben sandwich

An all-time favourite of New York delicatessens.

INGREDIENTS

225g (8oz) sauerkraut
8 slices of rye bread
4 tbsp bottled Russian dressing or Thousand Island salad dressing
8 slices of salt beef, about 30g (1oz) each
8 slices of Swiss cheese, thinly sliced, or Emmental cheese, thickly sliced
4 tbsp butter

METHOD

1 Place the sauerkraut in a sieve and rinse with cold water. Let it drain, pressing it down with a small plate.

2 Lay out 4 slices of bread. Top each with ½ tablespoon of dressing, 2 salt beef slices, a quarter of the sauerkraut, and 2 slices of cheese. Spread ½ tablespoon of dressing on each of the remaining bread slices, then place them, dressing-side down, on top.

3 Melt 1 tbsp of the butter in a large frying pan, add the sandwiches, in 2 batches, and cook over a medium-low heat for 2–3 minutes, or until the bottom slices are toasted, pressing the sandwiches down with a plate.

4 Carefully turn the sandwiches over, add 1 tbsp of butter, and cook for a further 2–3 minutes, or until the bottom slice is toasted and the cheese is melted. Cook the other sandwiches and serve while still warm.

GOOD WITH Sweet and sour pickles.

serves 4

prep 5 mins
• cook 8–12 mins

Quesadillas with ham, gherkin, and smoked cheese

Northern European flavours give this Latin snack an interesting twist.

INGREDIENTS

4 tbsp olive oil
8 wheat or corn tortillas
300g (10oz) smoked cheese
or strong mature Cheddar, grated
500g (1lb 2oz) cooked ham, sliced
8 gherkins, sliced
salt and freshly ground black pepper

METHOD

1 Heat the oil in a non-stick frying pan, then fry one tortilla for 1 minute or until golden.

2 Sprinkle 75g (2½oz) of the cheese over, leaving a little room around the edge. Top with 125g (4½oz) of the ham and 2 gherkins, then season with salt and pepper.

3 Top with the other tortilla, pressing it down with the back of a fish slice to sandwich the two together. Scoop the quesadilla up, carefully turn it over, and cook the other side for another minute, or until it is golden and the cheese melted. Repeat with the remaining tortillas. Slice in halves or quarters, and serve.

GOOD WITH A tomato salsa or relish.

makes 4

prep 5 mins
• cook 5 mins

Ribollita

This Tuscan soup was traditionally re-boiled (*ribolitta* in Italian) from the day before, giving it its name.

INGREDIENTS

2 tbsp olive oil
2 onions, finely chopped
salt and freshly ground black pepper
4 garlic cloves, grated or finely chopped
4 carrots, finely chopped
8 tomatoes, skinned and roughly chopped
2 x 400g cans cannellini beans, drained and rinsed
450g (1lb) potatoes, peeled and
cut into bite-sized pieces
350g (12oz) cavolo nero or curly kale, chopped
1.4 litres (2½ pints) hot vegetable stock
1 tbsp rosemary leaves, finely chopped
½ ciabatta, cut into cubes, to serve
drizzle of olive oil, plus extra to serve
Parmesan cheese, freshly grated, to serve

METHOD

1 Preheat the oven to 200°C (400°F/Gas 6). Heat the oil in a large pan, add the onions, and cook over a low heat for 6–8 minutes, or until soft and translucent. Season with salt and pepper, add the garlic and carrots, and cook for 5 minutes.

2 Stir through the tomatoes, beans, potatoes, and cavolo nero or curly kale, and cook for 5 minutes. Pour in the stock, add the rosemary, and simmer on a low heat for 15–20 minutes, or until the potatoes are soft. Taste, and season again with salt and pepper.

3 Place the ciabatta cubes on a baking tray, drizzle with olive oil, and bake in the oven for 10 minutes, or until golden. Serve the Ribollita topped with the ciabatta, a drizzle of olive oil, and a sprinkling of Parmesan cheese.

PREPARE AHEAD This soup will improve in flavour if made a day ahead; complete steps 1 and 2, cover, and chill. To reheat, transfer to a saucepan and heat until piping hot before serving with the ciabatta and cheese.

serves 8

prep 20 mins
• cook 40 mins

healthy option

freeze for
up to 3 months

CASSEROLES AND BAKES

Peel and dice an onion

Once an onion is halved, it can be sliced or diced. This technique is for quick dicing, which helps prevent your eyes from watering.

1 Using a sharp chef's knife, cut the onion lengthways in half and peel off the skin, leaving the root to hold the layers together.

2 Lay one half cut-side down. Make a few slices into the onion horizontally, cutting up to but not through the root.

3 With the tip of your knife, start to slice down through the layers vertically, cutting as close to the root as possible.

4 Cut across the vertical slices to produce even-sized dice. Use the root to hold the onion steady, then discard it when all the onion is diced.

Peel and chop garlic

Garlic is essential to many recipes, and peeling and preparing it is easy once you know how. Before you start, separate the cloves from the bulb.

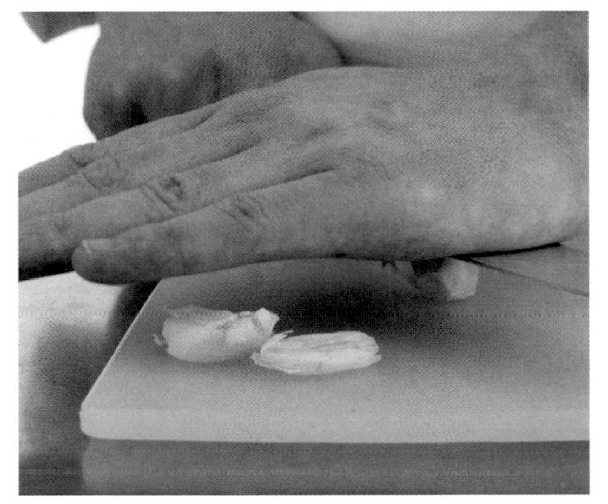

1 Place the garlic clove flat on a cutting board. Place a large knife blade on top and press it hard with the heel of your palm. Discard the skin.

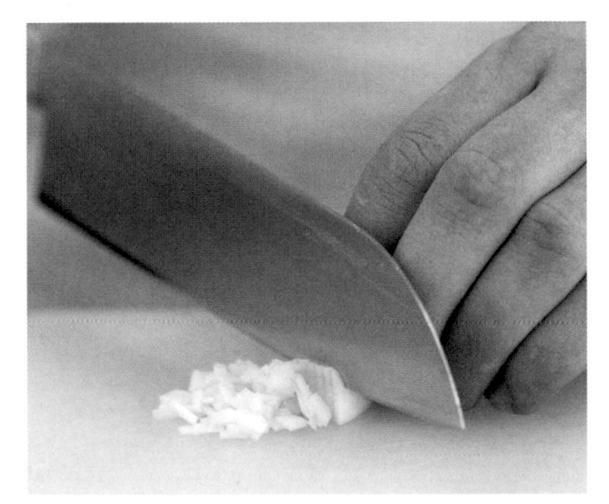

2 Slice the clove into slivers lengthways, then cut across to make tiny chunks. Gather the pieces into a pile and chop again for finer pieces.

Chop herbs

Use a large, sharp knife to chop fresh herbs just before you use them to release their flavour and aroma.

1 Strip the leaves from their stems and gather them together in a tight pile. With basil leaves (shown), layer the leaves and roll them gently.

2 Chop through the pile of herbs using a rocking motion with the knife. Gather again and repeat to achieve the desired size.

Courgette, herb, and lemon tagine

A flavourful vegetarian version of the famous Moroccan speciality.

INGREDIENTS

2 tbsp olive oil
2 red onions, finely chopped
salt and freshly ground black pepper
4 garlic cloves, grated or finely chopped
pinch of fennel seeds
pinch of ground cinnamon
2–3 tsp harissa (depending on taste), plus extra to serve
4 preserved lemons, halved, pith removed, and halved again
2 x 400g cans whole tomatoes, chopped
1 head of broccoli, broken into florets
6 courgettes, sliced
juice of 1 lemon
handful of dill, finely chopped
400g (14oz) couscous
handful of flat-leaf parsley, finely chopped
lemon wedges, to serve

METHOD

1 Heat half the oil in a large heavy-based pan, add the onions, and cook over a low heat for 8 minutes, or until soft and translucent. Season well with salt and pepper. Stir through the garlic, fennel seeds, cinnamon, harissa, and preserved lemons.

2 Add the tomatoes and stir well, crushing them with the back of a wooden spoon. Bring to the boil, then reduce to a simmer, and cook over a low heat for 30–40 minutes. If the sauce starts to dry out, top up with a little hot water.

3 Cook the broccoli in a pan of boiling salted water for 3–5 minutes or until tender, then drain and refresh in cold water. Drain again and put to one side. Heat the remaining oil in another frying pan, add the courgettes, and season with salt and pepper. Cook over a low heat, stirring frequently, for 5 minutes, or until they start to colour a little. Add the lemon juice and stir the dill through.

4 Meanwhile, put the couscous in a large bowl and pour over just enough boiling water to cover it. Leave for 10 minutes, then fluff up with a fork, and season well with salt and pepper. Add the broccoli and courgettes to the sauce, and stir through the parsley. Serve with the couscous, lemon wedges, and a spoonful of harissa.

serves 8

prep 25 mins • cook 1 hr

healthy option

Provençal lamb

This French-style big-pot dish requires little effort and will keep a hungry horde happy.

INGREDIENTS

4 tbsp olive oil
4 onions, cut into eighths
1.1kg (2½lb) lamb (from the leg), cut into bite-sized pieces
2 tsp paprika
6 garlic cloves, chopped
6 tbsp black olives
2 tbsp capers
4 tsp dried oregano
2 tsp dried thyme
6 tbsp fino sherry or dry sherry
salt and freshly ground black pepper
4 x 400g cans chopped tomatoes

METHOD

1 Preheat the oven to 150°C (300°F/Gas 2). Heat the oil in a large flameproof casserole over a medium-high heat, add the onions, and cook for 5 minutes, or until starting to soften. Add the lamb and paprika, and cook, turning frequently, for 8–10 minutes, or until the lamb is no longer pink.

2 Add the garlic, olives, capers, oregano, thyme, and sherry, and cook for 3 minutes. Season well with salt and pepper, add the tomatoes, stir well, and bring to the boil. Cover the pan with a well-fitting lid and transfer to the oven to cook for 2½ hours.

GOOD WITH Herbed mashed potatoes and olive oil.

serves 8

prep 25 mins • cook 2 hrs 30 mins

flameproof casserole

freeze for up to 3 months

Spanish-style chicken with pine nuts

Slow-cooked in wine and tomatoes, this chicken is deliciously tender.

INGREDIENTS

2 tbsp olive oil
8 chicken thighs
1 onion, finely chopped
salt and freshly ground black pepper
3 garlic cloves, grated or finely chopped
6 ripe tomatoes, skinned and chopped
1 small glass of red wine
900ml (1½ pints) hot chicken stock
handful of pine nuts, toasted
handful of sultanas (optional)

METHOD

1 In a large flameproof casserole, heat 1 tbsp of the olive oil over a medium-high heat. Add the chicken pieces, and brown for 5–8 minutes on each side until they are golden all over. Remove from the pan, and set aside.

2 Reduce the heat to medium. Add the remaining oil, the onion, and a pinch of salt to the same pan, and sweat the onions for about 5 minutes until soft.

3 Add the garlic and tomatoes, and season with pepper. Cook for a few minutes until the tomatoes are starting to break down. Add the red wine, increase the heat slightly, and simmer for a few minutes.

4 Pour in the hot stock, and bring to the boil. Reduce the heat to low, and return the chicken to the pan along with the pine nuts and sultanas (if using). Gently simmer for 30–40 minutes. Top up with a little hot water if it gets too dry. Serve hot.

GOOD WITH Rice or boiled new potatoes.

serves 4

prep 10 mins
• cook 1 hr

large flameproof casserole

Pork and bean stew

Otherwise known as *Feijoada*, this is the national dish of Brazil and is made with a variety of meats.

INGREDIENTS

500g (1lb 2oz) dried black-eyed beans
2 pig's trotters
250g (9oz) smoked pork ribs
175g (6oz) smoked streaky bacon, left in 1 piece
200g can chopped tomatoes
1 tbsp tomato purée
1 bay leaf
salt and freshly ground black pepper
oil, for frying
500g (1lb 2oz) lean pork fillet or steaks
1 small onion, finely chopped
2 garlic cloves, finely chopped
175g (6oz) chorizo, cut into small chunks
1 green chilli, deseeded (optional)
1 orange, cut into wedges, to garnish
3 spring onions, chopped, to garnish

METHOD

1 Rinse the beans, place them in a bowl, and pour over enough cold water to cover. Leave overnight.

2 Drain the beans and place in a large saucepan. Cover with fresh water, bring to the boil, and boil for 10 minutes, skimming off any scum, then lower the heat, cover, and simmer for 1 hour.

3 Meanwhile, place the pig's trotters, pork ribs, and streaky bacon in a saucepan with the canned tomatoes and their juice, the tomato purée, bay leaf, and salt and pepper to taste. Add enough cold water to cover, bring to the boil, skim off any scum, cover, reduce the heat, and simmer for 50 minutes.

4 Drain the cooked beans and reserve the cooking liquid, then return the beans to the pan. Add the meats with their cooking liquid. Add just enough of the reserved cooking liquid from the beans to cover. Continue to cook, covered, over a low heat, for a further 20 minutes.

5 Heat 1 tbsp of oil in a frying pan and brown the pork fillet. Add to the meat and bean mixture, and continue to cook for a further 10 minutes, or until the meat is tender and the beans very soft. Wipe out the frying pan, add 1 tbsp of oil, and fry the onion and garlic over medium heat for 3–4 minutes, stirring frequently, until soft and translucent. Add the chorizo and chilli, if using, and fry for a further 2 minutes, stirring. Add 2–3 tbsp of the cooked beans to the frying pan and mash well with the back of a spoon. Add the contents of the frying pan to the meat and beans, stir, and cook for a further 10 minutes.

6 To serve, remove the larger pieces of meat and cut into smaller pieces. Transfer them and the rest of the meat and bean mixture on to a serving dish, and garnish with orange wedges and spring onions. Serve immediately.

GOOD WITH Plain boiled rice, steamed or fried shredded kale, and a tomato salsa.

PREPARE AHEAD The stew can be made a day in advance and reheated.

serves 6–8

prep 1 hr 15 mins, plus soaking • cook 1 hr 35 mins

soak the beans overnight

Hungarian goulash

This warming winter stew makes a great main course if you are entertaining, as all the hard work can be done in advance.

serves 4

prep 25 mins • cook 2 hrs 30 mins

healthy option

freeze, without the soured cream, for up to 3 months

INGREDIENTS

4 tbsp oil
900g (2lb) braising steak, cut into 2.5cm (1in) cubes
2 large onions, thinly sliced
2 garlic cloves, crushed
2 red peppers, deseeded and chopped
1 tbsp paprika, plus extra to garnish
400g can chopped tomatoes
2 tbsp tomato purée
1 tbsp plain flour
300ml (10fl oz) beef stock
1 tsp chopped thyme
salt and freshly ground black pepper
150ml (5fl oz) soured cream

METHOD

1 Preheat the oven to 160°C (325°F/Gas 3). Heat half the oil in a large frying pan and brown the meat in batches, transferring to a large casserole as they finish browning.

2 Add the remaining oil to the pan, lower the heat, and fry the onions, garlic, and peppers until soft. Stir in the paprika and cook for 1 minute, then add the tomatoes and their juice, and tomato purée. Mix the flour with a little stock until smooth, then pour it into the pan with the rest of the stock. Bring to the boil, stirring often. Add the thyme, season to taste with salt and pepper, then pour the sauce into the casserole.

3 Cover tightly and place in the oven for 2 hours, or until the beef is very tender.

4 To serve, spoon the goulash into individual bowls and top each serving with a couple of spoonfuls of soured cream and sprinkle with a little paprika.

GOOD WITH Buttered tagliatelle.

Chicken with cider and cream

This casserole is simple to make but a treat to eat.

INGREDIENTS

1 tbsp olive oil
2 onions, cut into 8 wedges
salt and freshly ground black pepper
2 garlic cloves, grated or finely chopped
8 chicken thighs
300ml (10fl oz) cider
300ml (10fl oz) double cream
a few sprigs of rosemary, to garnish

METHOD

1 Preheat the oven to 200°C (400°F/Gas 6). Heat the olive oil in a large flameproof casserole over a low-medium heat. Add the onion and a pinch of salt, and sweat for 5 minutes until soft and translucent. Then add the garlic, and cook for 10 seconds.

2 Push the onions to one side of the casserole, and increase the heat to medium-high. Add a little more oil if needed, and put the chicken thighs in the casserole skin-side down. Brown for about 5 minutes on each side until golden.

3 Increase the heat slightly, and pour in the cider. Let boil for a few minutes, then reduce the heat to a simmer, and add the cream. Add the rosemary sprigs, and season well with salt and pepper.

4 Cover with a lid, and transfer to the oven to cook for about 40 minutes. If it is becoming too dry, add a little hot water or hot chicken or vegetable stock.

GOOD WITH Mashed potatoes and fresh crusty bread, to mop up the juices.

Aduki bean stew

Sweet, nutty aduki beans give this stew its body and texture.

INGREDIENTS

1 tbsp olive oil
1 onion, finely chopped
salt
2 garlic cloves, grated or finely chopped
½–1 tsp cayenne pepper
400g can aduki beans, drained and rinsed
400g can chopped plum tomatoes
500ml (16fl oz) hot vegetable stock
about 12 black olives, pitted

METHOD

1 Heat the olive oil in a pan over a low heat. Add the onion and a pinch of salt, and sweat gently for about 5 minutes until soft and translucent. Add the garlic and cayenne pepper to taste, and stir through.

2 Tip in the aduki beans and tomatoes, including any juices, and pour the stock over. Bring to the boil, then reduce the heat to low.

3 Simmer gently for 15–20 minutes, stirring through the olives for the last 5 minutes of cooking. If the stew dries out too much, top up with a little hot water.

GOOD WITH A crisp salad, new potatoes, or rice.

serves 4

prep 10 mins • cook 30 mins

healthy option

freeze for up to 3 months

Braised oxtail in wine with winter herbs

This wholesome winter dish is best served with a mound of buttery mash.

INGREDIENTS

3kg (6½lb) oxtail, cut into 225g (8oz) pieces
flour, for dusting
2 tbsp olive oil
1 tbsp clear honey
2 tbsp chopped thyme
2 tbsp chopped rosemary
salt and freshly ground black pepper
2 onions, chopped
1 fennel bulb, diced
2 carrots, cut into large chunks
2 garlic cloves, sliced
2 red chillies, finely chopped
750ml bottle full-bodied red wine
parsley, chopped, to garnish

METHOD

1 Preheat the oven to 150°C (300°F/Gas 2). Toss the oxtail in flour to lightly dust. Heat a large frying pan with the olive oil. Fry the oxtail, browning well on all sides.

2 Remove the oxtail and place in a large casserole. Drizzle the honey over the meat, scatter over the herbs, and season to taste with salt and pepper.

3 Add the vegetables, garlic, and chilli to the frying pan and fry for 6 minutes, or until slightly softened. Add to the oxtail and pour the wine over. Cover tightly and cook for 2–3 hours. The meat should fall away from the bone easily when cooked. Serve garnished with parsley.

GOOD WITH Creamy mashed potatoes.

serves 6

prep 20 mins
• cook 2–3 hrs

freeze for up to
3 months

Quick fish pie

Homely and filling, this pie is a British classic. It could also be made with any leftover seafood and mashed potatoes.

INGREDIENTS

900g (2lb) floury potatoes, peeled and quartered
knob of butter
675g (1½lb) white fish, such as haddock, hake, sustainable cod, or pollack, cut into chunky pieces
salt and freshly ground black pepper
150ml (5fl oz) milk
175g (6oz) frozen peas
4 hard-boiled eggs, peeled and chopped (optional)

For the sauce

30g (1oz) butter
30g (1oz) plain flour
300ml (10fl oz) milk
1 tbsp Dijon mustard
salt and freshly ground black pepper

METHOD

1 Preheat the oven to 200°C (400°F/Gas 6), or the grill to high. Boil the potatoes in a pan of salted water for about 15 minutes until soft. Drain well, and mash. Add the butter, and mash again. Set aside.

2 Put the fish in a shallow frying pan. Season well with salt and pepper. Pour over just enough of the milk to cover, and poach over a medium heat for 3–4 minutes. Remove the fish with a slotted spoon, and transfer to an ovenproof dish.

3 To make the sauce, melt the butter in a pan over a low heat. Remove from the heat, and stir in the flour with a wooden spoon until smooth. Return the pan to the heat, and add the milk little by little, stirring constantly. Keep cooking and stirring for 5–10 minutes until the sauce has thickened. Add more milk if needed. Stir through the mustard, and season with salt and pepper. Add the peas and eggs (if using) to the sauce, and stir gently.

4 Spoon the sauce on top of the fish, and stir gently. Top with the reserved mashed potatoes, and fork the top so that the potato forms peaks. Dot with a little extra butter if you wish, then cook in the oven or under a hot grill for about 10 minutes until the top is crisp and golden.

PREPARE AHEAD The potatoes and fish could be cooked the day before and kept chilled until needed. Bring the mashed potato back to room temperature before using it to top the pie.

serves 4

prep 15 mins
• cook 20 mins

freeze for up to
3 months

Chicken with pancetta, peas, and mint

Sweet peas, white wine, and fragrant mint give this dish a taste of summer.

serves 4

prep 15 mins • cook 1 hr 45 mins

large flameproof casserole

INGREDIENTS

2 tbsp olive oil
4 large or 8 small chicken pieces, such as thighs and breasts, skin on
2 onions, finely chopped
200g (7oz) pancetta, cubed, or bacon lardons
2 garlic cloves, grated or finely chopped
2 glasses of dry white wine
600ml (1 pint) hot chicken stock
salt and freshly ground black pepper
225g (8oz) frozen peas
handful of flat-leaf parsley, finely chopped
handful of mint leaves, finely chopped

METHOD

1 Preheat the oven to 150°C (300°F/Gas 2). Heat 1 tbsp of the oil in a large flameproof casserole (preferably cast-iron) over a medium heat. Add the chicken pieces, and cook for about 8 minutes until golden all over. Remove from the casserole, and set aside.

2 Reduce the heat to low, and add the remaining oil and onions to the casserole. Sweat gently for about 5 minutes until soft and translucent, then add the pancetta or bacon. Increase the heat a little, and cook for a further 5 minutes until the pancetta or bacon is golden. Stir in the garlic, then pour in the wine. Increase the heat to high, and simmer for a few minutes until the alcohol has evaporated.

3 Add the stock, and bring to the boil once again. Season with salt and pepper, add the peas, and stir through. Return the chicken pieces to the casserole. Stir through the parsley and mint, cover with a lid, and transfer to the oven to cook for 1½ hours. Check the level of liquid occasionally while cooking – it needs to be fairly dry, but if it does need topping up, just add a little hot water. Serve hot.

GOOD WITH Fresh, crusty bread or sautéed potatoes.

Chickpea and vegetable stew

This dish tastes better the next day as the flavours mature – simply reheat any leftovers.

INGREDIENTS

1 tbsp olive oil
1 onion, finely chopped
salt and freshly ground black pepper
2 garlic cloves, grated or finely chopped
3 celery sticks, finely chopped
3 carrots, finely chopped
1 small glass of white wine
400g can chopped plum tomatoes
150ml (5fl oz) hot vegetable stock
400g can chickpeas, drained and rinsed
handful of fresh runner beans or green beans, sliced diagonally

METHOD

1 Heat the oil in a large wide pan over a low heat. Add the onion and a pinch of salt, and sweat gently for about 5 minutes until soft and translucent. Stir in the garlic, celery, and carrots, and cook gently for a further 5 minutes.

2 Increase the heat, add the wine, and let boil until the alcohol has evaporated. Tip in the tomatoes, bring to the boil, and pour in the stock. Add the chickpeas, reduce the heat slightly, and simmer gently for 15 minutes.

3 Add the beans to the stew, and cook for 10 minutes more until soft. Season well with salt and pepper.

serves 4

prep 15 mins • cook 35 mins

healthy option

freeze for up to 3 months

Beef and leek couscous

Filling enough to be served as a main course, this is a convenient dish for feeding a hungry crowd.

INGREDIENTS

8 tbsp olive oil
6 leeks, finely sliced
675g (1½lb) minced beef
2 red chillies, deseeded and finely chopped
2 tsp paprika
6 garlic cloves, sliced
150ml (5fl oz) dry white wine
450ml (15fl oz) hot beef stock
handful of flat-leaf parsley, finely chopped
450g (1lb) couscous

METHOD

1 Preheat the oven to 150°C (300°F/Gas 2). Heat the oil in a large flameproof casserole, add the leeks, and cook over a medium heat for 5 minutes. Add the mince and cook, stirring occasionally, for 10 minutes, or until no longer pink.

2 Stir in the chillies, paprika, and garlic, and cook for 2 minutes. Pour in the wine and cook for 3 minutes, then add the stock and parsley, and combine well. Stir in the couscous, then cover with a lid, and cook in the oven for 15 minutes. Stir well and serve.

serves 6–8

prep 25 mins • cook 30 mins

large flameproof casserole

Smoked fish and anchovy gratin

A creamy and flavourful fish dish with a crisp, golden topping.

serves 4

prep 10 mins • cook 30 mins

healthy option

INGREDIENTS

250g (9oz) smoked fish, such as mackerel and salmon
8–12 whole anchovies in oil, drained
4 waxy potatoes, peeled, boiled, and sliced
knob of butter, melted

For the sauce

knob of butter
1 onion, finely chopped
1 garlic clove, grated or finely chopped
1 tbsp plain flour
300ml (10fl oz) milk
salt and freshly ground black pepper
handful of curly-leaf parsley, finely chopped

METHOD

1 Preheat the oven to 200°C (400°F/Gas 6). To make the sauce, melt the butter in a pan over a low heat. Add the onion, and sweat gently for about 5 minutes until soft and translucent, then add the garlic, and cook for a few seconds more. Remove from the heat, and stir through the flour using a wooden spoon, then add a little milk, and beat until smooth.

2 Return the pan to the heat, and slowly add the rest of the milk, stirring until the sauce has thickened. Season well with salt and pepper, and stir through the parsley.

3 Layer the smoked fish and anchovies in an ovenproof dish, then spoon over the sauce, and gently combine. Top with a layer of potatoes, brush with melted butter, and bake in the oven for 15–20 minutes until golden, crispy, and heated through.

GOOD WITH A crisp green salad.

Spicy lamb with baby potatoes

Warm, North African flavours enliven this dish.

serves 6–8

prep 25 mins • cook 1 hr 30 mins

large flameproof casserole

INGREDIENTS

675g (1½lb) lean lamb, cut into 2cm (¾in) cubes
3 tsp paprika
1 tsp cayenne pepper
zest of 2 lemons
10 tbsp olive oil
3 onions, finely diced
1.1kg (2½lb) small potatoes, such as Anya
large handful of flat-leaf parsley, finely chopped
6 garlic cloves, grated or finely chopped
2 tbsp thyme, finely chopped
1 tbsp rosemary leaves, finely chopped
6 preserved lemons, quartered and pith removed
salt and freshly ground black pepper

METHOD

1 Preheat the oven to 150°C (300°F/Gas 2). Put the lamb, paprika, cayenne, and lemon zest in a mixing bowl, combine well, then put to one side. Heat 4 tbsp of the oil in a large flameproof casserole, add the onions, and cook over a medium heat for 3 minutes. Add the lamb and cook, stirring frequently, for 5 minutes, or until no longer pink.

2 Add the potatoes and cook for 2 minutes, then add the parsley, garlic, thyme, rosemary, preserved lemons, and the rest of the olive oil. Combine well, season with salt and pepper, and cover with a lid. Place in the oven and cook, stirring frequently, for 1½ hours.

GOOD WITH Herbed couscous or rice.

Beef and tomato lasagne

A dollop of pesto perks up the flavours in this family favourite.

INGREDIENTS

6 tbsp olive oil
3 large onions, finely diced
675g (1½lb) lean minced beef
6 garlic cloves, chopped
3 tbsp tomato purée
3 x 400g cans chopped tomatoes
2 tsp dried oregano
3 bay leaves
salt and freshly ground black pepper
3 tsp pesto
50g (1¾oz) butter
3 heaped tbsp plain flour
1 litre (1¾ pints) milk
300g (10oz) Cheddar cheese, grated
450g (1lb) lasagne sheets

METHOD

1 Heat the oil in a large heavy-based pan over a medium heat, add the onions, and cook, stirring occasionally, for 5 minutes, or until starting to soften. Add the beef and cook, stirring constantly, for 5 minutes, or until no longer pink. Add the garlic, cook for 1 minute, then stir in the tomato purée. Add the tomatoes, oregano, and bay leaves, bring gently to the boil, then reduce the heat and simmer for 20 minutes. Season well with salt and pepper, remove from the heat, then stir through the pesto, and put to one side.

2 Melt the butter in a pan over a low heat, add the flour, and stir well. Add a little of the milk, mix well, then add 150ml (5fl oz) more milk, stirring vigorously until smooth. Add the rest of the milk, combine well, then bring to the boil, stirring constantly. Reduce the heat and simmer for 2 minutes to ensure the flour is cooked. Remove from the heat, stir in the Cheddar cheese, then season with salt and pepper.

3 Preheat the oven to 180°C (350°F/Gas 4). Pour 1cm (½in) of the beef sauce into the bottom of a large ovenproof dish. Cover with a layer of lasagne sheets, then add 1cm (½in) more beef sauce, followed by a small amount of the cheese sauce, and a layer of lasagne sheets. Repeat until all the meat sauce has been used up. Make sure you have enough cheese sauce for an even 5mm (¼in) layer on the top.

4 Cook in the oven for 35–40 minutes, or until brown on top. Serve while piping hot.

serves 8

prep 30 mins • cook 35–40 mins

freeze for up to 3 months

GOOD WITH A green leafy salad drizzled with olive oil and balsamic vinegar.

PREPARE AHEAD This recipe serves 8, so is perfect if you want to divide it and freeze some. Assemble the lasagne in an ovenproof freezerproof dish, as in Step 3, then let it cool completely before double-wrapping in cling film and freezing. To serve, remove the cling film and put it straight in an oven preheated to 180°C (350°F/Gas 4) for 35–40 minutes, or until piping hot.

Sausage and mustard casserole

This casserole is pure winter bliss. For an added twist, try it with a variety of sausages.

INGREDIENTS

1 tbsp olive oil
12 good-quality pork sausages
1 large onion, thinly sliced
225g (8oz) small chestnut mushrooms
1 cooking apple, peeled, cored, and cut into chunks
1 bay leaf
1 tbsp chopped sage
300ml (10fl oz) chicken stock
2 tsp Dijon mustard
1 tsp wholegrain mustard
1 tsp English mustard
150ml (5fl oz) double cream
salt and freshly ground black pepper

METHOD

1 Heat the oil in a large flameproof casserole and gently fry the sausages until golden all over. Remove the sausages with a slotted spoon and set aside.

2 Add the onion to the casserole and cook until softened. Add the mushrooms and cook for 5 minutes, then stir in the apple, bay leaf, sage, and stock.

3 Bring to the boil, then return the sausages to the casserole. Reduce the heat, cover, and cook gently for 20 minutes, stirring often. The apple pieces should break down and thicken the sauce slightly. If they are still holding their shape, mash them with the back of a wooden spoon and stir in.

4 Mix the mustards and cream together in a bowl, and season with salt and pepper. Pour into the casserole, increase the heat, and boil for 5 minutes, or until the sauce has thickened slightly.

GOOD WITH Creamy mashed potatoes and steamed cabbage.

serves 6

prep 15 mins
• cook 45 mins

large flameproof casserole

Spiced bean and herb hash

This medley of chopped potatoes and chilli beans makes a hearty breakfast or brunch.

INGREDIENTS

1 tsp olive oil
knob of butter
1 red onion, roughly chopped
salt and freshly ground black pepper
handful of thyme sprigs, leaves picked
450g (1lb) floury potatoes, peeled and cubed
400g can chilli mixed beans
150ml (5fl oz) hot vegetable stock
handful of flat-leaf parsley, finely chopped

METHOD

1 Heat the oil and butter in a non-stick frying pan over a low heat. Add the onion, a pinch of salt, and the thyme leaves, and sweat for about 5 minutes until the onion is soft.

2 Add the potatoes, and sauté until beginning to turn golden – you may need to add more olive oil.

3 When the potatoes are nearly cooked – after about 15 minutes – tip in the mixed beans, and stir together. Pour in the hot stock, and simmer for 10 minutes. Stir through the parsley, and season well with salt and pepper. Serve hot.

serves 4

prep 10 mins
• cook 30 mins

healthy option

freeze for up to 3 months

Baby courgettes with fish and couscous

Wholesome and hearty, this dish nevertheless has fresh, zesty flavours that you can enjoy in summer.

INGREDIENTS

8 tbsp olive oil
600g (1lb 5oz) baby courgettes, halved lengthways
zest and juice of 2 limes
3 tbsp tomato purée
1 tsp five-spice powder
1 tsp cayenne pepper
2 tsp paprika
1 tsp freshly ground black pepper
large handful of flat-leaf parsley, finely chopped
4 garlic cloves, grated or finely chopped
550g (1¼lb) white fish, such as haddock, cut into chunky bite-sized pieces
450ml (15fl oz) hot vegetable stock
450g (1lb) couscous

METHOD

1 Preheat the oven to 150°C (300°F/Gas 2). Put 2 tbsp of the oil in a bowl, add the courgettes, and mix well until evenly coated. Fry in a hot ridged cast-iron grill pan for 2 minutes on each side, then put to one side. You may need to do this in batches.

2 Add the rest of the oil to the bowl, together with the lime juice and zest, tomato purée, five-spice powder, cayenne, paprika, pepper, parsley, and garlic. Mix well, then add the fish, stock, couscous, and courgettes, and combine carefully.

3 Transfer to an ovenproof dish and cover with foil. Cook in the oven for 20 minutes, then stir well, and serve.

serves 6–8

prep 20 mins • cook 25 mins

healthy option

ridged cast-iron grill pan

STIR-FRIES

Spicy garlic green vegetable medley

A quick, Asian-inspired vegetarian stir-fry.

INGREDIENTS

handful of hazelnuts
1 tbsp sesame oil or vegetable oil
2 green chillies, deseeded and finely chopped
3 garlic cloves, thinly sliced
1 tbsp dark soy sauce
1 tbsp Chinese rice wine
1–2 heads of pak choi, quartered lengthways
handful of spinach or Swiss chard
2 handfuls of sugarsnap peas or mangetout, sliced into strips
salt and freshly ground black pepper

METHOD

1 Spread the hazelnuts over a baking tray. Toast under a hot grill until golden brown, turning them frequently. Put the hazelnuts in a clean tea towel, and rub off the skins. Roughly chop, and set aside.

2 Heat the oil in a wok over a medium-high heat, and swirl it around to coat the surface. Add the chillies and garlic, and cook for 10 seconds, then add the soy sauce and Chinese rice wine, and cook for a few seconds more.

3 Add the pak choi and spinach or Swiss chard, and stir-fry for a minute. Add the sugarsnap peas or mangetout, and stir-fry for a minute more. Toss, and season with salt and pepper. Serve immediately with the hazelnuts scattered over the top.

GOOD WITH Hot, fluffy rice.

serves 4

prep 15 mins • cook 15 mins

healthy option

wok

Pork and spring greens

Get the most from your roast – this is a perfect dish for using up leftovers.

INGREDIENTS

1 tbsp olive oil
350g (12oz) cooked pork, roughly shredded
4 garlic cloves, sliced
2 heads of spring greens, shredded
2 tsp onion seeds
salt and freshly ground black pepper

METHOD

1 Heat the oil in a wok over a medium-high heat. When the oil is hot, add the cooked pork. Stir-fry for about 5 minutes, moving the pork around the wok.

2 Add the garlic and greens, and continue to stir-fry over a medium-high heat for about 1 minute, until the greens have just wilted. Add the onion seeds, and stir to combine, then season well with salt and pepper. Serve immediately.

GOOD WITH Hot, fluffy rice.

serves 4

prep 10 mins • cook 10 mins

healthy option

wok

Crispy rice noodles with beef

This tasty dish is a combination of crunchy textures and Asian flavours.

INGREDIENTS

groundnut oil, for frying
140g (5oz) dried rice vermicelli
2 tbsp oyster sauce
3 tbsp dark soy sauce
1 tbsp soft brown sugar
350g (12oz) sirloin steak, sliced
2 garlic cloves, thinly sliced
1 tsp grated ginger
12 thin asparagus spears, cut into 2.5cm (1in) lengths
6 spring onions, cut into 2.5cm (1in) lengths
toasted sesame oil, for drizzling
2 tbsp roasted cashews, chopped

METHOD

1 Heat 5cm (2in) groundnut oil in a deep-fat fryer or large saucepan to 190°C (375°F) or until a piece of stale bread browns in less than 1 minute. Snip the vermicelli into short lengths and deep-fry in batches for a few seconds, or until white and crisp. Remove and drain well on kitchen paper. Keep warm.

2 Mix the oyster sauce, soy sauce, sugar, and 1 tbsp water. Set aside. Heat 2 tbsp groundnut oil in a wok over a high heat and stir-fry the beef for 2 minutes, or until browned. Remove and set aside.

3 Add a little more groundnut oil, and stir-fry the garlic and ginger for 30 seconds. Add the asparagus and spring onions, stir-fry for 2 minutes, then add the sauce, and return the beef to the wok. Cook for 1 minute, then drizzle with sesame oil.

4 Pile the stir-fry on top of the vermicelli, scatter with the cashews, and serve immediately.

serves 4

prep 20 mins
• cook 15 mins

deep-fat fryer or
large saucepan
• wok

Hokkien noodles with char-sui pork

Char-sui is pork fillet marinated in hoisin, oyster sauce, and red pepper, then barbecued to give it a shiny scarlet glaze.

INGREDIENTS

45g (1½oz) dried Chinese mushrooms, such as Cloud Ear
2 tbsp oyster sauce
2 tbsp light soy sauce
1 tsp clear honey
2 tbsp groundnut oil or vegetable oil
2 garlic cloves, crushed
2 tsp finely grated fresh root ginger
1 red pepper, deseeded and finely sliced
140g (5oz) mangetout, halved lengthways
500g (1lb 2oz) fresh Hokkien noodles (thick egg noodles)
350g (12oz) char-sui pork, thinly sliced

METHOD

1 Put the mushrooms in a heatproof bowl, cover with boiling water, and set aside for 30 minutes to soak. Strain and cut the mushrooms into thin strips.

2 Simmer a large pan of water ready to cook the noodles. In a cup or small bowl, mix together the oyster sauce, soy sauce, and honey.

3 Heat the oil in a wok or large frying pan. Stir-fry the garlic and ginger for 30 seconds. Add the red pepper, stir-fry for 3 minutes, then add the mangetout and mushrooms, and stir-fry for 1 minute.

4 Drop the noodles into the pan of simmering water and cook for 1 minute, or until tender. Meanwhile, add the pork to the wok, pour in the oyster sauce mixture, and toss over the heat for 1 minute, until everything is combined and piping hot. Drain the noodles, mix with the stir-fried pork and vegetables, and serve at once.

serves 4

prep 20 mins, plus soaking • cook 10 mins

Parsi eggs

This Indian dish has its origins in ancient Persia.

INGREDIENTS

60g (2oz) unsalted butter
4 spring onions, thinly sliced
1 tsp grated fresh root ginger
1 large red or green chilli, deseeded and finely chopped
2 tsp mild curry powder
4 tomatoes, deseeded and chopped
8 large eggs
2 tbsp milk
salt and freshly ground black pepper
2 tbsp chopped coriander

METHOD

1 Melt 30g (1oz) of the butter in a large non-stick frying pan and fry the onions, ginger, and chilli over a low heat for 2 minutes, or until softened, stirring often.

2 Add the curry powder and tomatoes, and cook for 1 minute. Remove from the pan and set aside.

3 Add the rest of the butter to the pan. Beat the eggs and milk, and season with salt and pepper. Pour into the pan, and stir until scrambled and almost set. Add the curried vegetables, stir well, and cook until just set. Scatter the chopped coriander over, and serve at once.

GOOD WITH Salad leaves, lightly toasted naan bread, or chapatis.

serves 4

prep 10 mins
• cook 15 mins

Patatas bravas

Translated as "fierce potatoes", this is a spicy Spanish tapas dish.

INGREDIENTS

6 tbsp olive oil
700g (1lb 9oz) white potatoes, peeled and cut into 2cm ($^{3}/_{4}$in) cubes
2 onions, finely chopped
1 tsp chilli flakes
2 tbsp dry sherry
zest of 1 lemon
4 garlic cloves, grated or finely chopped
200g can chopped tomatoes
handful of flat-leaf parsley, chopped
salt and freshly ground black pepper

METHOD

1 Preheat the oven to 200°C (400°F/Gas 6). Heat half the oil in a non-stick frying pan, add the potatoes, and cook, turning frequently, over a medium-low heat for 20 minutes, or until starting to brown. Add the onions and cook for a further 5 minutes.

2 Add the chilli flakes, sherry, lemon zest, and garlic and allow to reduce for 2 minutes before adding the tomatoes and parsley. Season with salt and pepper, combine well, and cook over a medium heat for 10 minutes, stirring occasionally.

3 Add the remaining oil, place the contents of the frying pan in a shallow baking dish, and cook in the oven for 30 minutes, or until cooked. Serve hot.

GOOD WITH A selection of tapas dishes (try Chorizo with peppers, page 130).

serves 4

prep 15 mins • cook 1 hr

Chorizo with peppers

A Spanish-style snack with robust flavours.

INGREDIENTS

2 tbsp olive oil
2 red peppers, deseeded and cut into 2cm (3/4in) squares
2 green peppers, deseeded and cut into 2cm (3/4in) squares
3 garlic cloves, crushed
300g (10oz) chorizo cut into 2cm (3/4in) cubes
2 tbsp dry sherry
1 tsp dried oregano
salt and freshly ground black pepper

METHOD

1 Heat the oil in a frying pan, add the peppers, and cook over a medium heat, stirring occasionally, for 5 minutes. Add the garlic, chorizo, and sherry, and cook for 5 minutes more.

2 Sprinkle over the oregano, season with salt and pepper, and serve.

GOOD WITH Toasted ciabatta or other country-style bread as a quick supper or snack, or with other tapas-style dishes (try Patatas bravas, page 128).

Potato and horseradish hash

Fantastic for brunch, this recipe can also be a handy use for leftover potatoes.

INGREDIENTS

450g (1lb) floury potatoes, peeled
1 tbsp olive oil
knob of butter
200g (7oz) bacon rashers, chopped
3 tsp creamed horseradish
salt and freshly ground black pepper
250g (9oz) curly kale, cooked and chopped

METHOD

1 Boil the potatoes in a pan of salted water for 15–20 minutes until soft. Drain, then cut into bite-sized pieces, or mash, if you like.

2 Heat the olive oil and butter in a large non-stick frying pan over a medium heat. When the butter has melted, add the bacon rashers. Fry for 5–6 minutes until golden and crispy. Tip in the potatoes and stir through. Add the horseradish cream, and season with salt and pepper. Stir through the curly kale until everything is combined. Cook for a few minutes until lightly golden and a little crispy. Serve hot.

GOOD WITH Red cabbage.

PREPARE AHEAD You can cook the potatoes in step 1 the day before; keep chilled until ready to use.

PIES AND TARTS

Make shortcrust pastry

Shortcrust is the most versatile pastry, suitable for both tarts and pies. The quantities here suit most recipes.

1 Sieve 225g (8oz) of plain flour into a large bowl, and add a pinch of salt. Cut 125g ($4^1/_2$oz) of butter into small cubes, and add to the flour. For best results, use chilled butter.

2 Rub the butter lightly into the flour using your fingertips, lifting the mixture as you go. The more air you incorporate, the lighter the pastry. Continue rubbing until the mixture resembles breadcrumbs.

3 Add about 2 tablespoons of cold water and use a round-bladed knife to bring the ingredients together. Work gently to bind the flour into the mixture.

4 Gather the pastry into a ball using your fingertips. If it is too dry and crumbly, add a little water until it comes together. Cover the pastry with cling film, and chill in the refrigerator for 30 minutes.

Line a tart tin

Follow these steps to line any size and shape of tin. Use chilled pastry, straight from the refrigerator (see left).

1 Roll out the pastry on a lightly floured surface, to a circle about 5cm (2in) wider than the tart tin. The pastry should be fairly thin.

2 Carefully drape the pastry over a rolling pin and gently lay it over the tart tin, so the pastry hangs over the edge on all sides.

3 Gently ease the pastry into the sides of the tin using your fingertips or knuckles, being careful not to tear it.

4 Prick the base all over with a fork, then roll a rolling pin over the top of the tin to cut away the excess pastry. Chill for 30 minutes before baking.

Bake pastry blind

A pastry case for a tart or pie must be pre-cooked if its filling will not be baked, or baked only for a short time.

1 Fit the pastry in the tin and ensure that you prick the bottom thoroughly with a fork (see p137). This will allow trapped air to escape during baking and prevent the pastry from rising.

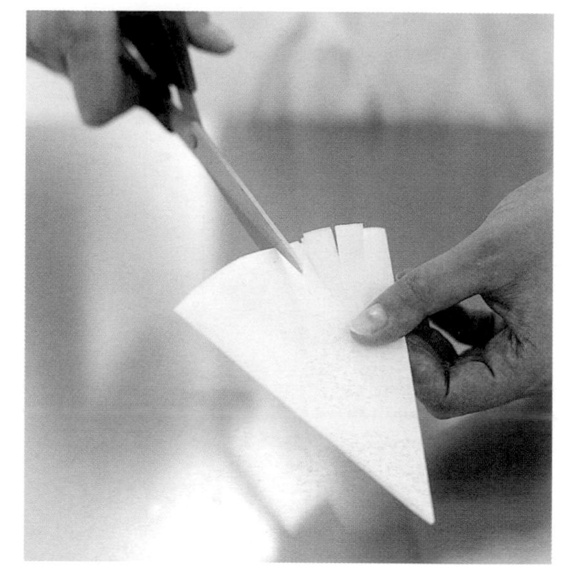

2 Cut out a circle of baking parchment, just slightly larger than the tin. Fold the parchment in half 3 times to make a triangular shape and clip the edge at regular intervals with scissors.

3 Place the parchment circle into the tin and fill it with an even layer of ceramic or metal baking beans. Bake at 180°C (350°F/ Gas 4) for 15–20 minutes – it will be partially baked.

4 When cool enough to handle, remove the parchment and beans. Allow to cool slightly before adding the filling and return to the oven to cook fully according to the recipe's instructions.

Decorate and seal pastry

Before baking tarts and pies, remove excess pastry, and decorate the edges for a finished look. For pies, use beaten egg white to seal in moisture.

The forked edge gives an attractive finish and is simple to achieve. Use a fork to press the pastry to the rim of the base. Repeat around the edge of the rim at even intervals.

For a rope edge, pinch the pastry between your thumb and the knuckle of your index finger, then place your thumb in the groove left by the index finger, and pinch as before. Repeat around the edge.

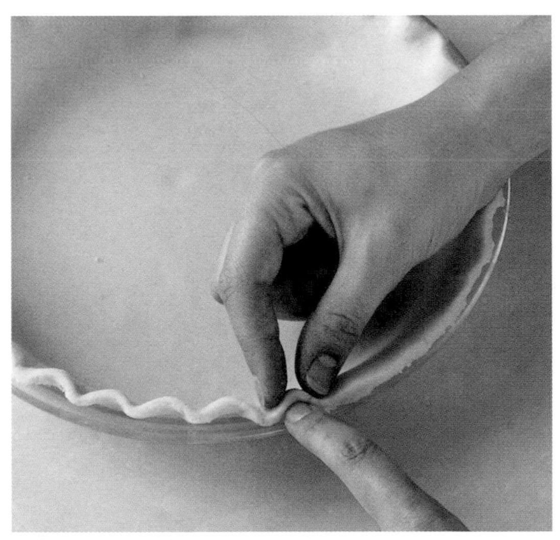

For a fluted edge, push one index finger against the outside edge of the rim and pinch the pastry with the other index finger and thumb to form a ruffle. Repeat around the edge.

To seal a pie, make sure you press the pastry lid firmly to the base. Use beaten egg white to strengthen the seal and to give the top of the pie a glossy finish.

Sausage and tomato tart

Sweet, juicy tomatoes are a lovely partner for rich, savoury sausagemeat.

INGREDIENTS

225g (8oz) ready-made shortcrust pastry
flour, for dusting
1 egg, lightly beaten
½ tbsp olive oil
1 onion, finely chopped
salt and freshly ground black pepper
400g (14oz) good-quality pork sausages, skinned
1 tsp dried oregano
4 tomatoes, sliced

METHOD

1 Preheat the oven to 200°C (400°F/Gas 6). Roll out the pastry on a floured work surface, and use to line the pie dish or tart tin. Trim away any excess, line the pastry shell with greaseproof paper, and fill with baking beans. Bake in the oven for 15–20 minutes until the edges are golden. Remove the beans and paper, brush the bottom of the pastry with a little of the beaten egg, and return to the oven for 2–3 minutes to crisp. Remove from the oven, and set aside. Reduce the oven temperature to 180°C (350°F/Gas 4).

2 Meanwhile, heat the oil in a large frying pan over a low heat. Add the onion and a pinch of salt, and sweat gently for about 5 minutes until soft and translucent. Add the sausagemeat, breaking it up with a fork or the back of a spatula. Season well with salt and pepper, and sprinkle the oregano over. Cook, stirring regularly, over a low-medium heat for about 10 minutes until no longer pink. Leave to cool, then mix in the remaining egg.

3 Spoon the sausage mixture into the pastry shell, then layer the tomatoes over the top. Bake in the oven for about 20 minutes until lightly golden. Leave to cool for about 10 minutes, then slice in the dish or tin.

GOOD WITH A crisp green salad.

serves 4

prep 15 mins, plus cooling • cook 60 mins

20cm (8in) square pie dish or fluted tart tin • baking beans

Goat's cheese tartlets

Individual oat pastry cases are the perfect container for a light tangy goat's cheese and yogurt filling, for a starter or light lunch.

serves 4

prep 25 mins, plus chilling • cook 35–40 mins

4 loose-bottomed tartlet tins 12.5cm (5in) in diameter and 2.5cm (1in) deep • baking beans

INGREDIENTS

2 large eggs
90ml (3fl oz) Greek yogurt
150ml (5fl oz) milk
2 tbsp snipped chives
salt and freshly ground black pepper
85g (3oz) goat's cheese, crumbled

For the pastry

85g (3oz) plain flour, plus extra for dusting
pinch of salt
25g (scant 1oz) rolled oats
60g (2oz) butter, chilled and diced

METHOD

1 To make the pastry, sift the flour and salt into a large mixing bowl, and stir in the oats. Add the butter and rub in until the mixture resembles breadcrumbs. Sprinkle with 2 tablespoons of cold water and mix in, using a round-bladed knife. Gather the dough together and lightly knead on a floured surface for a few seconds, or until smooth. Wrap in cling film and chill for 30 minutes.

2 Preheat the oven to 200°C (400°F/Gas 6) and place a baking tray inside. Divide the pastry dough into 4 pieces. Roll out each one thinly on a lightly floured surface and use to line the tartlet tins. Prick the pastry bases several times with a fork, and line each with a piece of foil and baking beans. Bake for 10 minutes, then remove the foil and beans, and return to the oven for 5 minutes. Remove from the oven and reduce the oven temperature to 180°C (350°F/Gas 4).

3 Whisk the eggs, yogurt, milk, chives, and salt and pepper in a jug. Divide the cheese between the pastry cases, then carefully pour over the egg mixture. Bake for 20–25 minutes, or until the filling is lightly set and beginning to brown.

4 Leave to cool slightly, then remove from the tins, and serve warm, or at room temperature.

GOOD WITH Salad leaves and toasted pine nuts.

PREPARE AHEAD Make the pastry and line the tartlet tins up to 1 day in advance. If serving cold, the tartlets can be refrigerated, and covered with cling film, for up to 48 hours.

Smoked mackerel and spring onion tart

A wholesome, affordable fish, smoked mackerel gives this tart a rich flavour.

INGREDIENTS

250g (9oz) ready-made shortcrust pastry
flour, for dusting
2 eggs, plus 1 extra for egg wash
1 tbsp olive oil
1 bunch of spring onions, finely chopped
salt and freshly ground black pepper
2 smoked mackerel fillets, about 100g (3½oz) each, skinned and flaked
200ml (7fl oz) crème fraîche
handful of flat-leaf parsley, finely chopped
1 bunch of chives, finely chopped

METHOD

1 Preheat the oven to 200°C (400°F/Gas 6). Roll out the pastry on a floured work surface, and use to line the tart tin. Trim away the excess, line the pastry shell with greaseproof paper, and fill with baking beans. Bake in the oven for 15–20 minutes until the edges are golden. Remove the beans and paper, brush the bottom of the shell with a little of the egg wash, and return to the oven for 2–3 minutes to crisp. Remove from the oven, and set aside. Reduce the oven temperature to 180°C (350°F/Gas 4).

2 Heat the oil in a small frying pan over a low heat. Add half of the spring onions and a pinch of salt, and sweat gently for about 5 minutes. Spoon evenly over the bottom of the pastry shell along with the remaining uncooked spring onion. Scatter over the mackerel, and season with plenty of pepper.

3 Mix together the crème fraîche and the 2 eggs. Add the parsley and chives, and season with a little salt. Mix through. Carefully pour over the tart filling, then bake in the oven for 20–30 minutes until set and golden. Leave to cool for 10 minutes before releasing from the tin.

GOOD WITH A fresh tomato and cucumber salad.

serves 4

prep 15 mins • cook 50 mins

18cm (7in) round loose-bottomed straight-sided tart tin • baking beans

Vegetable samosas

In India, ghee (clarified butter) is used to make these pastries, but oil works just as well.

INGREDIENTS

450g (1lb) potatoes
225g (8oz) cauliflower, chopped into small pieces
175g (6oz) peas, thawed if frozen
3 tbsp vegetable oil or ghee
2 shallots, sliced
2 tbsp curry paste or powder
2 tbsp chopped coriander leaves
1 tbsp lemon juice
salt and freshly ground black pepper

For the pastry

350g (12oz) plain flour, plus extra for dusting
1/2 tsp salt
6 tbsp vegetable oil or ghee, plus extra for frying

METHOD

1 To make the pastry, sift the flour into a bowl with 1/2 tsp of salt. Stir in the oil or ghee and gradually add 120ml (4fl oz) warm water, mixing to make a dough.

2 Knead the dough on a floured surface until smooth. Wrap in cling film and leave to rest for at least 30 minutes.

3 To make the filling, cook the unpeeled potatoes in a saucepan of boiling water until tender. Drain and, when cool enough to handle, peel and chop into small pieces.

4 Blanch the cauliflower florets in a pan of boiling water for 2–3 minutes, or until just tender, then drain. If using fresh peas, blanch them with the cauliflower.

5 Heat the oil in a large frying pan and fry the shallots for 3–4 minutes, stirring frequently, until soft. Add the potatoes, cauliflower, peas, curry paste or powder, coriander, and lemon juice, season to taste, and cook over a low heat for 2–3 minutes, stirring occasionally. Set aside to cool.

6 Divide the dough into 8 equal pieces. Roll them out so each forms an 18cm (7in) round. Cut each round in half and shape into a cone, dampening the edges to seal. Spoon a little of the filling into each cone, dampen the top edge of the dough, and press down over the filling to enclose it. Repeat with the rest of the dough and filling.

7 Heat oil in the deep-fat fryer to 180°C (350°F) and fry the samosas in batches for 3–4 minutes, or until golden brown on both sides. Drain on kitchen paper and serve hot or cold.

GOOD WITH A bowl of chutney or raita.

PREPARE AHEAD The samosas can be prepared 1 day in advance, chilled, and fried just before serving.

serves 4

prep 45 mins, plus resting and cooling • cook 35–40 mins

deep-fat fryer or large saucepan, half-filled with oil

freeze, uncooked, for up to 1 month

Stuffed filo tartlets

A stylish appetizer that is great for entertaining.

INGREDIENTS

12 sheets filo pastry, 40 x 30cm (16 x 12in)
olive oil, for brushing and drizzling
3 red peppers or orange peppers, deseeded, and cut into quarters
300g (10oz) chorizo sausage, sliced
½ red onion, peeled and finely sliced
150g (5½oz) goat's cheese or feta cheese, crumbled

METHOD

1 Preheat the oven to 180°C (350°F/Gas 4). Brush each filo sheet with oil and cut in half. Place 4 sheets on top of each other in the tin, oiled-sides down, giving each a quarter turn. Push the sides into the edge of the tin. Bake for 10 minutes, or until the pastry is crisp. Set aside.

2 Preheat the grill on its highest setting. Grill the peppers until blackened all over, and place in a plastic bag to cool. Slip off the skins and thickly slice the peppers.

3 Heat a frying pan with a tiny drizzle of olive oil and fry the chorizo until crisp. Drain.

4 Arrange the peppers, onion, and cheese on the tarts. Top with hot chorizo to serve.

serves 6

prep 45 mins • cook 20 mins

6 loose-bottomed tartlet tins

Empanadas

These savoury Spanish pastries make very versatile nibbles.

INGREDIENTS

1 tbsp olive oil
1 onion, finely chopped
120g can whole tomatoes, drained
2 tsp tomato purée
140g can tuna, drained
2 tbsp finely chopped flat-leaf parsley

For the pastry

450g (1lb) plain flour, plus extra for dusting
salt and freshly ground black pepper
85g (3oz) butter, diced
2 eggs, beaten, plus extra to glaze

METHOD

1 To make the pastry, sift the flour into a large mixing bowl with 1/2 tsp salt. Add the butter and rub in with your fingertips until it resembles fine breadcrumbs. Add the beaten eggs with 4–6 tbsp water and combine to form a dough. Cover with cling film and chill for 30 minutes.

2 Meanwhile, heat the oil in a frying pan, add the onion, and fry over a medium heat, stirring often, for 5–8 minutes, or until translucent. Add the tomatoes, tomato purée, tuna, and parsley, and season to taste with salt and pepper. Reduce the heat and simmer for 10–12 minutes, stirring occasionally.

3 Preheat the oven to 190°C (375°F/Gas 5). Roll out the pastry to a thickness of 3mm (1/8 in). Cut out 24 rounds with a pastry cutter. Put 1 tsp of the filling on each, then brush the edges with water, fold over, and pinch together.

4 Place the empanadas on an oiled baking tray and brush with beaten egg. Bake for 25–30 minutes, or until golden brown. Serve warm.

makes 24

prep 45 mins, plus chilling • cook 40–50 mins

9cm (3½in) round pastry cutter

Cheese and onion tart

Anchovies give a salty kick to this mildly flavoured onion tart.

INGREDIENTS

350g ready-made shortcrust pastry
flour, for dusting
2 tbsp olive oil
30g (1oz) butter
450g (1lb) onions, thinly sliced
750g (1lb 10oz) curd cheese
120ml (4fl oz) milk
2 large eggs
1 tsp cumin seeds or caraway seeds, crushed (optional)
salt and freshly ground black pepper
60g (2oz) anchovy fillets, halved lengthways

METHOD

1 Roll out the pastry thinly on a lightly floured board, then use to line the tin. Chill for 30 minutes.

2 Heat the oil and butter in a pan, and add the onions. Cover and cook over a gentle heat, stirring occasionally, for 20 minutes, or until the onions are soft but not browned. Uncover and cook for a further 4–5 minutes, or until golden. Set aside to cool.

3 Preheat the oven to 200°C (400°F/Gas 6). Line the pastry case with greaseproof paper and baking beans, and bake blind for 15 minutes. Remove the beans and paper, and bake for a further 10 minutes.

4 Reduce the oven temperature to 180°C (350°F/Gas 4). Spoon the onions into the pastry case, spreading them in an even layer. Beat together the curd cheese, milk, eggs, and cumin or caraway seeds, if using. Season to taste with salt and pepper, then pour into the pastry case. Lay the anchovy fillets in a lattice pattern on top, and bake for 25 minutes, or until the pastry is golden and the filling is set. Serve warm.

PREPARE AHEAD This tart can be cooked up to 1 day in advance, covered, and chilled. Reheat in a hot oven for 10 minutes, or until completely warmed through.

serves 4–6

prep 15 mins, plus chilling and cooling • cook 1 hr 15 mins

20cm (8in) loose-bottomed fluted tart tin • baking beans

Cheesy spinach pie

This crisp spinach pastry or, *Spanakopita*, is popular in Greece.

INGREDIENTS

4 tbsp olive oil
1 onion, peeled and chopped
1 bunch of spring onions, chopped
900g (2lb) spinach, shredded
small bunch of dill, chopped, or 4 tsp dried dill
small bunch of flat-leaf parsley, chopped
225g (8oz) feta cheese, finely crumbled
4 eggs, beaten
freshly ground black pepper
150g (5½oz) butter, melted
250g (9oz) filo pastry or at least 14 sheets, about 40 x 30cm (16 x 12in), thawed if frozen

METHOD

1 Heat the olive oil in a large saucepan until hot and fry the onion and spring onions for 5 minutes, or until softened but not browned, stirring occasionally.

2 Add the spinach, mix well, cover, reduce the heat, and cook for 7–8 minutes, or until wilted, stirring occasionally.

3 Stir in the chopped herbs, increase the heat, and cook, uncovered, stirring, for 15 minutes, or until the liquid evaporates and the mixture starts to stick to the bottom of the saucepan. Transfer to a bowl lined with kitchen paper, and cool.

4 Remove the paper and stir in the cheese and beaten eggs. Season to taste with plenty of pepper.

5 Preheat the oven to 160°C (325°F/Gas 3). Thickly brush the cake or roasting tin with butter and line with a sheet of filo pastry, carefully pressing it into the sides and corners of the tin. Brush with butter and lay another sheet on top, pressing it down, as before. Continue this layering process until you have used half the pastry.

6 Spread the spinach mixture into the pastry case. Place another sheet of filo on top and brush with butter. Continue this process to use up the remaining sheets. Trim the excess pastry away from the side of the tin, using scissors. Brush the top with any remaining butter and bake in the centre of the oven for 1 hour, or until the pastry is crisp and golden brown all over.

7 Cut into squares and serve hot or slightly warm.

GOOD WITH Other Greek or Middle Eastern light dishes, such as hummus and taramasalata.

PREPARE AHEAD Rinse the spinach well under cold water. Shake well and pat dry using kitchen paper.

serves 12

prep 35 mins, plus cooling • cook 1 hr 30 mins

28 x 23 x 4cm (11 x 9 x 1½in) cake tin or small roasting tin

Feta and pumpkin pastries

These tasty, crisp Middle Eastern pastries have a sweet, spicy centre.

makes 24

prep 20 mins, plus cooling • cook 30 mins

INGREDIENTS

100g (3½oz) pumpkin or squash, peeled and deseeded
25g (scant 1oz) raisins, chopped
100g (3½oz) feta cheese, finely crumbled
freshly ground black pepper
½ tsp ground cinnamon
6 sheets filo pastry, 40 x 30cm (16 x 12in), thawed if frozen
50g (1¾oz) butter, melted, plus extra for greasing
flour, for dusting

METHOD

1 Finely dice the pumpkin flesh and place it in a small saucepan. Pour in enough water to just cover the pumpkin, bring to the boil, cover, and simmer gently for 5 minutes, or until tender. Drain well and allow to cool.

2 Preheat the oven to 180°C (350°F/Gas 4). Mix the pumpkin with the raisins and feta cheese. Season with pepper and add the cinnamon. Set aside.

3 Lay the filo sheets on top of each other and cut into 4 long strips, about 7.5cm (3in) wide. Stack the strips on top of each other and cover with dampened kitchen paper.

4 Taking 1 strip of pastry at a time, brush with butter, and place a heaped teaspoon of the pumpkin mixture 2.5cm (1in) from one end. Fold over the end of the strip of pastry to cover the filling.

5 Fold a corner of the pastry over diagonally to form a triangular pocket of filled pastry. Working upwards, keep folding diagonally, from one side to the other, to retain the triangular shape, until all the pastry is folded, making sure any gaps in the pastry are pressed closed.

6 Lightly dust the work surface with flour, and keep the triangles in a pile, covered with a damp cloth to stop them drying out, while preparing the other pastries.

7 Transfer the triangles to a greased baking tray. Brush with the remaining butter and bake for 20–25 minutes, or until crisp and golden. Serve while still warm.

GOOD WITH Other Greek or Middle Eastern dishes as part of a meze meal, or as a light snack or canapé.

PREPARE AHEAD The pastries can be prepared up to 24 hours in advance of baking, and chilled.

Ricotta and bacon tart

A simple, stylish tart with a light but smokey-flavoured filling.

INGREDIENTS

15g ($^1/_2$oz) butter
1 medium onion, chopped
115g (4oz) lean bacon, chopped into small pieces
250g (9oz) ricotta cheese
2 eggs
90ml (3fl oz) milk
3 tbsp freshly grated Parmesan cheese
1 tbsp snipped chives
1 tbsp chopped thyme
salt and freshly ground black pepper

For the pastry

175g (6oz) plain flour, plus extra for dusting
85g (3oz) butter, chilled and diced

METHOD

1 Sift the flour into a large bowl. Add the butter and rub into the flour, using your fingertips, until the mixture resembles coarse breadcrumbs. Add about 3 tablespoons of cold water and mix in with a knife to make a firm dough. Roll out the pastry on a floured surface and use it to line the tin. Chill for at least 20 minutes.

2 Heat the oven to 200°C (400°F/Gas 6). Put the tin on a baking tray, line with greaseproof paper and baking beans, and bake blind for 10 minutes. Remove the paper and beans, and bake for a further 5 minutes. Remove from the oven and allow to cool. Reduce the oven temperature to 180°C (350°F/Gas 4).

3 Meanwhile, melt the butter in a saucepan and add the onion. Cook over a low heat, covered, for 10–15 minutes, stirring occasionally, until soft and translucent. Remove the lid and add the bacon. Cook over a medium heat, stirring occasionally until the bacon is cooked through and colours slightly.

4 Mix the ricotta with the eggs and milk. Add the Parmesan and herbs, and season to taste with salt and pepper. Stir in the bacon and onion, and pour the mixture into the pastry case. Bake for 35 minutes, or until the filling has set. Leave to cool slightly in the tin, then transfer to a serving plate.

serves 4

prep 35 mins, plus chilling • cook 1 hr 10 mins

23cm (9in) flan tin • baking beans

freeze for up to 3 months

Gruyère tart

This vegetarian tart has a crisp, thyme-flavoured pastry.

INGREDIENTS

15g (1/2oz) butter
1 tbsp olive oil
1 large onion, thinly sliced
pinch of freshly grated nutmeg
1 tsp caster sugar
115g (4oz) Gruyère cheese, grated
3 eggs
100ml (3 1/2fl oz) double cream
60ml (2fl oz) milk
1 tsp Dijon mustard
salt and freshly ground black pepper

For the pastry

140g (5oz) plain flour, plus extra for dusting
60g (2oz) wholemeal flour
125g (4 1/2oz) butter, chilled and diced
1 tsp chopped thyme

METHOD

1 To make the pastry, mix the flours together in a large bowl. Using your fingertips, rub in the butter until the mixture resembles fine breadcrumbs. Stir in the thyme and sprinkle with 3–4 tablespoons of cold water. Mix with a round-bladed knife to make a firm dough. Knead on a lightly floured surface for a few seconds, until smooth. Shape into a slightly flattened ball and wrap in lightly oiled cling film. Chill for 30 minutes.

2 Meanwhile, heat the butter and oil in a large frying pan, add the onion, and fry over a low heat for 15 minutes, or until soft, stirring frequently. Stir in the nutmeg and sugar, then cook for a further 2–3 minutes, or until beginning to colour. Remove from the pan, and leave to cool.

3 Roll out the pastry on a lightly floured surface, and use it to line the tin. Chill for 15 minutes.

4 Place a baking tray in the oven and preheat to 200°C (400°F/Gas 6). Prick the pastry base all over with a fork, then line with greaseproof paper and baking beans. Bake for 15 minutes, then remove the paper and beans. Return to the oven for a further 5–10 minutes, or until crisp. Lower the oven temperature to 190°C (375°F/Gas 5).

5 Stir half the cheese into the cooled onion mixture, then spoon into the pastry case. Sprinkle with the remaining cheese. Beat together the eggs, cream, milk, and mustard in a jug, and season to taste with salt and pepper. Pour over the cheese and onions, and bake for 30 minutes, or until lightly set.

6 Leave to cool for 10 minutes, then carefully remove from the tin. Serve warm or cold.

GOOD WITH A rocket or watercress salad, with tomatoes, black olives, and a lemon-flavoured dressing.

PREPARE AHEAD Make the pastry and onion mixture up to 24 hours in advance, cover with cling film, and chill. Bring to room temperature before continuing.

serves 6

prep 25 mins, plus chilling • cook 45 mins

35 x 12cm (14 x 5in) tranche tin • baking beans

Olive, thyme, and onion tart

An easy-to-make tart – there is no need to blind bake the pastry case.

INGREDIENTS

3 tbsp olive oil
3 onions, finely sliced
1 tsp caster sugar
2 tbsp chopped thyme leaves
1 tsp salt
240ml (8fl oz) double cream
3 eggs, beaten
freshly ground black pepper
30g (1oz) Parmesan cheese, grated
2 tbsp black olive tapenade

For the pastry

115g (4oz) butter
3 tbsp milk
150g (5½oz) self-raising flour

METHOD

1 To make the pastry, heat the butter and milk together in a saucepan until the butter is melted. Stir in the flour and mix until a ball forms. When cool enough to handle, press the pastry into a 20cm (8in) loose-bottomed tart tin, and chill for 30 minutes.

2 Preheat the oven to 190°C (375°F/Gas 5). Heat the olive oil in a heavy frying pan, and add the onions, stirring, over a high heat for 5 minutes. Add the sugar, thyme, and salt, then reduce the heat, and cook slowly, stirring occasionally, for 30 minutes, or until the onions are very soft and slightly caramelized. Meanwhile, whisk together the cream and eggs, season with black pepper, and stir in the Parmesan.

3 Place the tart tin on a baking tray, and spread the tapenade over the base of the pastry. Spread the onions on top and carefully pour over the cream filling. Bake the tart for 30 minutes, or until set. Serve while still warm, or leave to cool completely and serve cold.

GOOD WITH A rocket salad dressed with a nutty vinaigrette.

PREPARE AHEAD The pastry case can be made 1 day in advance, and chilled until ready to serve.

serves 4–6

prep 40 mins, plus chilling • cook 30 mins

20cm (8in) loose-bottomed tart tin

Parmesan cheese and walnut tart

This nutty pastry works brilliantly with the creamy cheese filling.

INGREDIENTS

450ml (15fl oz) double cream
2 large eggs
2 large egg yolks
150g (5½oz) Parmesan cheese, grated
freshly ground black pepper
pinch of nutmeg

For the pastry

50g (1¾oz) walnut halves
225g (8oz) plain flour, plus extra for dusting
125g (4½oz) salted butter, chilled and diced

METHOD

1 Preheat the oven to 200°C (400°F/Gas 6). To make the pastry, pulse the walnuts in a food processor until finely ground, add the flour and butter until it resembles fine breadcrumbs, pour in 2–3 tbsp cold water, and pulse to a firm dough.

2 Roll the pastry on a floured surface and use to line the tart tin. Prick the base and chill for 30 minutes.

3 Place greaseproof paper and baking beans into the tart tin. Bake blind for 10 minutes, then remove the paper and beans, and cook for another 10 minutes to crisp the base. Lower the temperature to 180°C (350°F/Gas 4).

4 Beat the cream, whole eggs, and egg yolks together well. Stir in the Parmesan and some pepper and nutmeg. Pour into the pastry case and bake for 25 minutes, or until set. Allow it to stand for 10 minutes, then carefully remove the tart from the tin. Cut into slices and serve warm.

GOOD WITH Mixed leaves and a mild chutney, or tomato salad.

PREPARE AHEAD This tart can be made up to 2 days in advance, and chilled until ready to serve.

serves 6–8

prep 25 mins, plus chilling and standing • cook 45 mins

food processor • 23 × 23cm (9 × 9in) or 35 × 11cm (14 × 4½in) loose-bottomed tart tin • baking beans

freeze for up to 3 months

Sausage, bacon, and egg pie

This pie transports well and so is good for picnics.

INGREDIENTS

450g (1lb) sausagemeat or good-quality pork sausages, skinned
½ onion, finely chopped
pinch of nutmeg
pinch of mace
1 tbsp wholegrain mustard
salt and freshly ground black pepper
6 streaky, rindless bacon rashers
4 eggs
milk, to glaze

For the pastry

350g (12oz) plain flour, plus extra for dusting
175g (6oz) butter, chilled
salt and freshly ground black pepper
1½ tbsp tomato ketchup

serves 6–8

prep 15 mins, plus chilling • cook 50 mins

food processor • 20cm (8in) ovenproof pie dish 3.5cm (1½in) deep

METHOD

1 Make the pastry by placing the flour and butter in a food processor and pulsing until the mixture resembles breadcrumbs. Add the seasoning, ketchup, and 5–6 tbsp cold water, and pulse again, until it comes together in a ball. Wrap in lightly oiled cling film and chill for 30 minutes.

2 Preheat the oven to 200°C (400°F/Gas 6). Roll out half of the pastry fairly thinly on a lightly floured surface and line the pie dish.

3 Mix the sausagemeat with the onion, nutmeg, mace, and mustard, then season to taste with salt and pepper, and spread evenly over the base of the pie crust. Place the bacon over the sausagemeat in lines and crack the eggs over the bacon, leaving them intact if possible, as it looks nice when slicing the pie.

4 Roll out the remaining pastry, cover the pie, and pinch the edges to seal. Lightly score a criss-cross pattern on top and brush with a little milk.

5 Bake the pie for 20 minutes, then reduce the heat to 180°C (350°F/Gas 4), and bake for another 30 minutes. Cool before serving.

PREPARE AHEAD The pastry case can be made the day before and chilled; keep the lid pastry also chilled, then roll out when needed.

Steak and ale pie

Beer helps to tenderize the beef and imparts a delicious flavour.

INGREDIENTS

3 tbsp plain flour, plus extra for dusting
salt and freshly ground black pepper
675g (1½lb) lean braising steak, cut into 2cm (¾in) pieces
3 tbsp sunflower oil
1 large onion, chopped
1 garlic clove, crushed
115g (4oz) button mushrooms, halved
175ml (6fl oz) beef stock
175ml (6fl oz) brown ale
1 bay leaf
½ tsp dried thyme
1 tbsp Worcestershire sauce
1 tbsp tomato purée
350g (12oz) ready-made puff pastry
beaten egg or milk, to glaze

METHOD

1 Season the flour to taste with salt and pepper. Toss the steak in the flour, shaking off any excess.

2 Heat 2 tbsp of the oil in a large non-stick frying pan and fry the steak in batches over a high heat until browned on all sides. Transfer the steak to a large saucepan.

3 Add the remaining oil to the frying pan and fry the onion over a medium heat for 5 minutes. Add the garlic and mushrooms, and cook for 3–4 minutes, or until beginning to brown, stirring frequently.

4 Transfer the onion and mushrooms to the saucepan along with the stock, ale, bay leaf, thyme, Worcestershire sauce, and tomato purée. Bring to the boil, reduce the heat, cover, and simmer gently for 1 hour 30 minutes, or until the meat is tender.

5 Using a slotted spoon, transfer the meat and vegetables to the pie dish. Reserve 150ml (5fl oz) of the gravy and pour the rest over the meat mixture. Leave to cool.

6 Preheat the oven to 200°C (400°F/Gas 6). Roll out the pastry on a lightly floured surface to a thickness of 3mm (⅛in) and 5cm (2in) larger all round than the dish. Cut a 2cm (¾in) strip from around the pastry, brush the rim of the dish with water, and place the strip on the rim. Brush with water. Place the pastry over the dish and press the pastry edges together to seal; trim off the excess with a knife.

7 Crimp the pastry edge by using one index finger to make an indent on the outside rim and using the index finger and thumb of the other hand to pinch gently around the indent from the inside rim of the pastry to form a ruffle. Repeat around the pastry edge. Use the pastry trimmings to decorate, if you like. Brush the pastry with beaten egg and make a hole in the middle for steam to escape. Place on a baking tray and bake for 25 minutes, or until the pastry is puffed and dark golden. Serve immediately, with the reserved gravy served separately.

PREPARE AHEAD Make the filling up to 24 hours ahead and keep, covered, in the refrigerator until ready to make the pie.

serves 4

prep 20 mins, plus cooling • cook 2 hrs 15 mins

1.7-litre (3-pint) pie dish

Squash and Gorgonzola tart

Use either type of Gorgonzola cheese – dolce is creamy and piccante is firm with a fuller flavour.

INGREDIENTS

450g (1lb) squash, peeled and deseeded
olive oil
400g (14oz) spinach
2 large eggs
1 egg yolk
300ml (10fl oz) double cream
50g (1¾oz) Parmesan cheese, grated
nutmeg, grated
salt and freshly ground black pepper
115g (4oz) Gorgonzola cheese, crumbled

For the pastry

225g (8oz) plain flour
115g (4oz) butter, chilled
iced water

METHOD

1 For the pastry, put the flour and butter into a food processor, and pulse until it resembles breadcrumbs. Add just enough iced water to bind the pastry, then remove it from the machine, roll it out, and line the tin. Chill for 30 minutes.

2 Preheat the oven to 180°C (350°F/Gas 4). Prick the bottom of the tart case, line it with a circle of greaseproof paper, and add baking beans. Bake blind for 10 minutes, remove the paper and beans, and let it bake for another 10 minutes to crisp.

3 Slice the squash into thick slices, put on a roasting tray, and brush lightly with olive oil. Bake for 30 minutes, or until tender. Meanwhile, place the spinach and a little olive oil in a saucepan, and cook over a medium heat for 4 minutes. Drain and leave to cool. Whisk the eggs, egg yolk, cream, Parmesan, and nutmeg together, and season to taste with salt and pepper.

4 Squeeze the spinach dry and spread it across the bottom of the tart case, then add slices of squash and crumble over the Gorgonzola. Pour in the egg mixture and bake for 30–40 minutes, or until the filling is set. Remove from the oven and leave it to cool for 10 minutes before serving.

serves 6

prep 25 mins, plus chilling and cooling • cook 1 hr 30 mins

food processor • 20cm (8in) loose-bottomed flan tin • baking beans

freeze unbaked pastry case for up to 1 month

Steak and kidney pudding

A classic old English recipe that is just the dish for hearty appetites.

INGREDIENTS

675g (1½lb) lean stewing steak
200g (7oz) ox kidney
3 tbsp plain flour
salt and freshly ground black pepper
1 onion, chopped
150g (5½oz) mushrooms, quartered
2 tbsp Worcestershire sauce
200ml (7fl oz) beef stock

For the pastry

350g (12oz) self-raising flour
½ tsp salt
150g (5½oz) shredded suet

METHOD

1 To make the pastry, sift the flour and salt into a bowl, and stir in the suet. Make a well in the centre and stir in just enough cold water to mix to a soft, but not sticky, dough.

2 Trim off any excess fat from the steak and cut the steak and kidney into bite-sized pieces. Season the flour with salt and pepper, then toss the steak and kidney pieces in the flour to coat evenly. Combine with the onion and mushrooms.

3 Roll out ⅔ of the pastry and use to line the pudding bowl. Add the meat mixture, packing closely into the pastry-lined bowl. Sprinkle over the Worcestershire sauce, then add just enough stock to cover ¾ of the filling.

4 Roll out the remaining pastry to make a lid. Tuck the pastry edges around the pudding bowl inwards, brush with water, and place the pastry lid on top, pressing to seal.

5 Top the pudding bowl with a circle of pleated greaseproof paper, then top with a double layer of pleated foil. Tuck the foil around the rim of the basin firmly, or secure with string if necessary.

6 Place the bowl in the top of a steamer, or on an upturned saucer in a pan of boiling water to come halfway up the sides. Cover and steam for 4 hours, checking the level of water often to ensure it does not boil dry. To serve, remove the foil and greaseproof paper, run a knife around the edge of the pudding to loosen, then turn out on to a serving plate.

GOOD WITH A selection of winter vegetables, such as carrots, cabbage, or leeks.

PREPARE AHEAD The pastry can be made up to 1 day in advance, then wrapped and chilled until needed.

serves 6–8

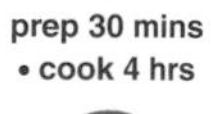

prep 30 mins • cook 4 hrs

1.5-litre (2¾-pint) pudding bowl

freeze for up to 3 months

Leek and cheese flamiche

A savoury puff pastry tart from the Burgundy and Picardy regions of France.

INGREDIENTS

400g (14oz) puff pastry
flour, for dusting
45g (1½oz) butter
500g (1lb 2oz) leeks, sliced
150g (5½oz) cream cheese
4 tbsp double cream
2 tbsp chopped chives
60g (2oz) Parmesan cheese, grated
pinch of nutmeg
freshly ground black pepper
1 egg yolk, beaten

METHOD

1 Preheat the oven to 200°C (400°F/Gas 6). Line a large baking tray with greaseproof paper. Cut the pastry in half and roll each piece into a 30 x 20cm (12 x 8in) rectangle. Place 1 piece on the baking tray and chill. Wrap the remaining piece in cling film and chill.

2 Melt the butter in a frying pan, add the leeks, and cook gently, stirring occasionally, for 15 minutes. Remove the pan from the heat and leave to cool.

3 Mix the cream cheese, cream, chives, Parmesan, nutmeg, and a pinch of pepper together and stir into the leeks. Remove the pastry from the fridge, spread the leek mixture across the base, leaving a 2cm (¾in) border of pastry all around the edge. Brush the border with egg yolk.

4 Place the pastry lid on top and pinch the edges together to seal. Brush the top with egg yolk. Make a few small cuts in the centre of the pie to allow steam to escape, and decorate the top with the point of a knife in a criss-cross pattern. Bake for 30 minutes, or until golden. Allow the flamiche to cool for 10 minutes before serving.

serves 6

prep 30 mins, plus chilling and cooling • cook 45 mins

freeze for up to 1 month

GOOD WITH A leafy green salad, or a tomato and onion salad.

PREPARE AHEAD This can be made up to 2 days in advance, covered in cling film and chilled.

Cheese and pepper jalousie

This puff pastry treat makes the most of ready-prepared ingredients.

INGREDIENTS

500g (1lb 2oz) puff pastry
flour, for dusting
3 tbsp sun-dried tomato purée
115g (4oz) mature Cheddar cheese, grated
280g jar sliced mixed peppers in oil, drained
115g (4oz) mozzarella, cut into 1cm (1/2in) dice, or grated
freshly ground black pepper
beaten egg or milk, to glaze

METHOD

1 Preheat the oven to 220°C (425°F/Gas 7). Roll out just less than half the pastry on a lightly floured surface to make a 30 x 15cm (12 x 6in) rectangle. Lay the pastry on a large dampened baking tray. Roll out the remaining pastry to a 30 x 18cm (12 x 7in) rectangle, lightly dust with flour, then fold in half lengthways. Make cuts 1cm (1/2in) apart along the folded edge to within 2.5cm (1in) of the outer edge.

2 Spread the tomato purée over the pastry on the baking tray to within 2.5cm (1in) of the edges, and top with the Cheddar. Pat the peppers with kitchen paper to remove excess oil, and arrange on top of the cheese. Scatter with the mozzarella and season to taste with pepper.

3 Dampen the edges of the pastry with water. Carefully place the second piece of pastry on top and press the edges together to seal; trim off the excess. Brush the top with beaten egg and bake for 25 minutes, or until golden brown and crisp. Leave to cool for a few minutes before slicing and serving.

GOOD WITH A mixed leaf salad.

Sweetcorn and pepper filo triangles

Filo, popular for its crispness and flakiness, is perfect for these vegetable-stuffed triangles.

INGREDIENTS

1 tbsp olive oil
1 onion, finely chopped
salt and freshly ground black pepper
3 red peppers, deseeded and diced
340g can sweetcorn, drained
175g (6oz) feta cheese, cut into small cubes
200g (7oz) filo pastry
a little butter, melted, plus extra for glazing

METHOD

1 Preheat the oven to 200°C (400°F/Gas 6). Heat the oil in a large frying pan over a low heat. Add the onion and a pinch of salt, and sweat gently for about 5 minutes until soft and translucent. Tip in the peppers, and continue cooking for a further 10 minutes until the peppers are soft. Stir through the sweetcorn and feta, and season well with black pepper.

2 Lay out the filo sheets into four piles of 3 or 4 layers about 30 x 10cm (12 x 4in), brushing each pile with a little melted butter. Divide the pepper mixture between each pile of pastry, spooning it on to the bottom right-hand corner of each one. Fold this corner so that it makes a triangle, then fold the top right-hand corner down. Repeat until you have made 5 folds in all for each one, and end up with 4 large triangles.

3 Brush the triangles all over with a little melted butter, and put them on an oiled baking tray. Bake in the oven for about 20 minutes until crisp and golden. Serve hot.

GOOD WITH A mixed leaf salad.

makes 4

prep 20 mins
• cook 20 mins

freeze for up to 3 months

Feta filo pie

Crisp pastry encases a delicious blend of spinach, feta, and pine nuts in this classic Middle Eastern dish.

INGREDIENTS

900g (2lb) fresh spinach leaves
100g (3½oz) butter
1 tsp ground cumin
1 tsp ground coriander
1 tsp ground cinnamon
2 red onions, finely chopped
60g (2oz) dried apricots, chopped
60g (2oz) pine nuts, toasted
6 sheets filo pastry, 40 x 30cm (16 x 12in), thawed if frozen
salt and freshly ground black pepper
300g (10oz) feta cheese, crumbled
flat-leaf parsley, to garnish
lemon zest, to garnish

METHOD

1 Rinse the spinach leaves, shake off the excess water, and pack into a large saucepan. Cover and cook over a medium heat for 8–10 minutes, turning occasionally, until just wilted. Drain well through a sieve or colander, pressing the spinach against the sides to extract as much water as possible. Set aside, still draining, to cool.

2 Meanwhile, melt 25g (scant 1oz) butter until bubbling and gently fry the spices with the onion over a low heat, stirring occasionally, for 7–8 minutes, or until softened but not browned. Stir in the apricots and pine nuts, then set aside. Preheat the oven to 200°C (400°F/Gas 6). Grease and line the springform tin.

3 To assemble the pie, melt the remaining butter. Brush the prepared tin with melted butter and cover the base with a sheet of pastry, leaving the edges overhanging, and brush with butter. Continue with 5 more sheets, brushing each with butter. Leave the edges overhanging.

4 Blot the cooled spinach with kitchen paper, then chop finely. Stir into the cooked onion mixture, and season to taste with salt and pepper. Pile half into the pastry case and spread evenly.

5 Sprinkle the cheese over the spinach, then cover with the remaining spinach mixture. Fold the overhanging pastry over the spinach, piece by piece, brushing with butter. Brush the top with any remaining butter and place the tin on a baking tray. Bake for 35–40 minutes, or until crisp and golden. Let it stand for 10 minutes before carefully releasing from the tin.

6 Serve hot or warm, cut into wedges, and garnish with parsley and strips of lemon zest.

GOOD WITH A crisp salad or seasonal vegetables.

serves 6

prep 30 mins, plus cooling and standing • cook 1 hr

20cm (8in) springform tin

PUDDINGS

Make crêpes

Making great crêpes involves two essentials – the right temperature and the perfect batter. See p212 for ingredient quantities.

1 Heat a little oil or clarified butter in a crêpe pan, or non-stick frying pan, and pour off any excess. Holding the pan at an angle, pour in a little of the batter.

2 Tilt and swirl the pan as you pour in more batter to coat the base of the pan thinly and evenly. Allow to cook gently until the surface starts to bubble.

3 Use a long spatula to loosen the crêpe. It should be a pale gold colour underneath. Flip the crêpe back into the pan to cook the other side.

4 Cook until the second side is golden. Place on baking parchment with a layer between each finished crêpe. Continue cooking the rest of the batter.

Make crumble

Adding a crumble to fresh fruit makes a quick dessert. Make sure the butter is chilled and your hands are cool. See p202 for ingredient quantities.

1 Rub unsalted butter into plain flour until it resembles chunky breadcrumbs. Add sugar and oats and mix together.

2 Cut fresh fruit to line the bottom of an ovenproof dish. Spoon over the crumble mixture, and bake until golden and crisp.

Core and peel apples

Choose apples that are sweet-smelling, firm, and unbruised. The skin should be taut and unbroken.

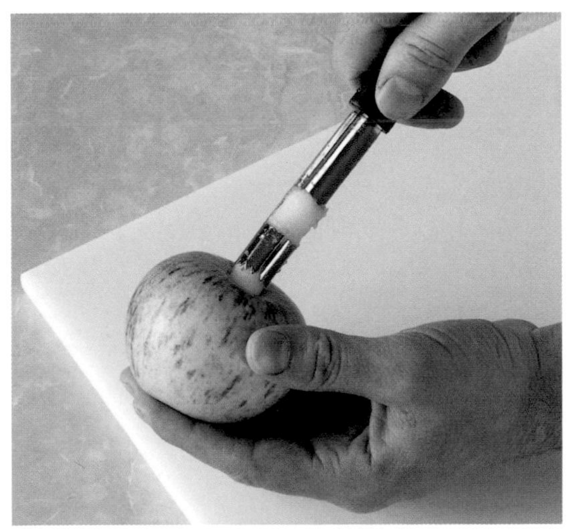

1 Core an apple by pushing a corer straight into the stalk of the apple and through to the bottom. Twist and loosen the core, then pull it out with the corer.

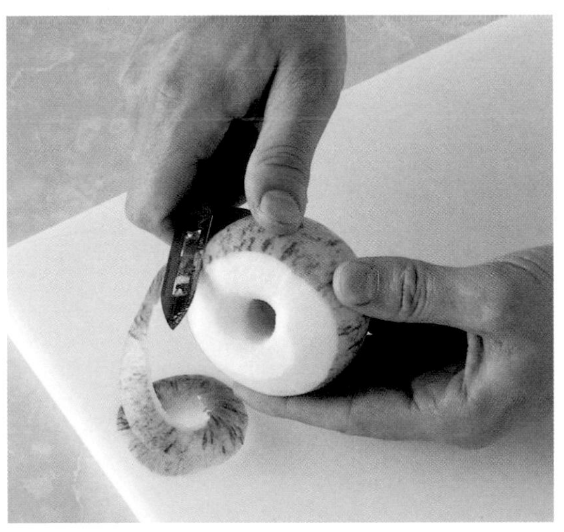

2 Using a peeler or small paring knife, gently remove the skin of the apple by making a circular path around the body from top to bottom.

Blueberry cobbler

A classic summer-fruit dessert.

INGREDIENTS

450g (1lb) blueberries
2 large peaches or 2 eating apples, sliced
grated zest of 1/2 lemon
2 tbsp caster sugar

For the cobbler

225g (8oz) self-raising flour
2 tsp baking powder
75g (2 1/2oz) caster sugar, plus 1 tbsp for sprinkling
pinch of salt
75g (2 1/2oz) butter, chilled and diced
1 egg
100ml (3 1/2fl oz) buttermilk
handful of flaked almonds

METHOD

1 Preheat the oven to 190°C (375°F/Gas 5). Spread the blueberries and peaches over the base of a shallow ovenproof dish, and sprinkle with lemon zest and sugar.

2 Sift the flour, baking powder, caster sugar, and salt into a bowl. Add the butter and work together with your fingers until the mixture resembles breadcrumbs.

3 Break the egg into the buttermilk and beat well. Add to the dry ingredients and mix together to form a soft, sticky dough. Drop walnut-sized spoonfuls of the mixture over the top of the fruit, leaving a little space between them. Press them down lightly with your fingers, then sprinkle over the flaked almonds and 1 tablespoon of sugar.

4 Bake for 30 minutes, or until golden and bubbling, covering it loosely with kitchen foil if it is browning too quickly. It is done when a skewer pushed into the middle comes out clean. Leave to cool briefly before serving.

GOOD WITH A spoonful of custard or double cream with each serving.

serves 4

prep 15 mins
• cook 30 mins

Apple Charlotte

This hot fruit dish was apparently created for Queen Charlotte.

INGREDIENTS

1.35kg (3lb) cooking apples, peeled, cored, and sliced
finely grated zest and juice of 1 lemon
85g (3oz) sultanas
115g (4oz) caster sugar
140g (5oz) butter
1 large loaf of white bread, unsliced
½ tsp ground cinnamon
icing sugar, to dust

METHOD

1 Place the apples in a large heavy saucepan with the lemon zest and juice, sultanas, and 85g (3oz) of the caster sugar. Cover and cook over a low heat, shaking the pan occasionally, for 8–10 minutes, or until the apples are very tender and beginning to fall apart.

2 Preheat the oven to 190°C (375°F/Gas 5). Melt the butter in a small saucepan, and brush a little on the base and sides of the cake tin. Remove the crusts from the bread, then cut the bread into 14 slices. Brush both sides of the bread slices with the butter. Mix together the remaining sugar and the cinnamon, and sprinkle over 1 side of each slice.

3 Use 3 slices of bread to cover the base of the tin, cutting the bread to fit and laying it sugar-side downwards. Cut 8 of the remaining slices in half and use to line the sides of the tin, sugar-side outwards, slightly overlapping them to fit.

4 Spoon the apple mixture into the bread case. Cover with the remaining slices, sugar-side upwards, cutting to fit if necessary. Fold over the bread on the sides of the tin so it slightly overlaps the top of the Charlotte. Bake uncovered for 30–35 minutes, or until crisp and golden. Leave to stand in the tin for at least 5 minutes before turning out on a plate. Dust with icing sugar to serve.

serves 6–8

prep 30 mins
• cook 40–45 mins

23cm (9in)
springform
cake tin

Tarte Tatin

This caramelized upside-down apple tart is a French classic.

INGREDIENTS

150g (5½oz) butter, softened
200g (7oz) caster sugar
6 large dessert apples, such as Granny Smith's, peeled, cored, and roughly chopped

For the pastry

150g (5½oz) butter
50g (1¾oz) sugar
225g (8oz) plain flour, plus extra for dusting
1 egg, beaten

METHOD

1 To make the pastry, cream the butter and sugar together until blended. Gradually mix in the flour, then stir in the egg to bind it together. Turn the mixture on to a lightly floured surface and knead until smooth. Wrap in cling film and chill for at least 1 hour.

2 Preheat the oven to 220°C (425°F/Gas 7). For the topping, melt the butter in a 30cm (12in) ovenproof tin over a medium heat. When the butter has melted, add the sugar, stirring occasionally. Increase the heat slightly until the mixture begins to bubble, then continue cooking, stirring occasionally, for 5 minutes, or until it is a light, toffee colour. Remove from the heat.

3 Arrange the apple pieces in the tin on top of the caramel mixture, rounded-side down and tightly packed together.

4 Roll out the pastry to form a circle just large enough to fit over the top of the apples. Arrange the pastry neatly on top of the fruit and tuck the edges into the tin. Bake for 30 minutes, or until the pastry is lightly browned and cooked. Allow the tart to stand for 10 minutes before carefully inverting on to a large serving plate. Serve while still warm.

GOOD WITH A spoonful of whipped cream, crème fraîche, or ice cream.

PREPARE AHEAD You can make the pastry up to 24 hours in advance, cover it with cling film, and refrigerate.

serves 8

prep 30 mins, plus chilling • cook 35 mins

30cm (12in) ovenproof tin or flameproof shallow round dish

Bread and butter pudding

Careful cooking in a low oven will produce a pudding with a smooth, velvety texture.

INGREDIENTS

30g (1oz) butter, plus extra to grease
5–6 slices of day-old bread, crusts removed, about 175g (6oz) in total
60g (2oz) raisins
3 eggs
300ml (10fl oz) full-fat milk
200ml (7fl oz) single cream
60g (2oz) caster sugar
1 tsp pure vanilla extract
4 tbsp apricot jam
2–3 tsp lemon juice

METHOD

1 Lightly grease an ovenproof dish with a little butter. Spread the remaining butter on the slices of bread. Cut each slice in half diagonally then in half again to form 4 triangles.

2 Place the raisins in the bottom of the dish and arrange overlapping slices of bread on the top. Beat together the eggs, milk, cream, sugar, and vanilla extract. Carefully pour the mixture over the bread and leave to soak for at least 30 minutes.

3 Preheat the oven to 180°C (350°F/Gas 4). Place the dish in a deep roasting tin and pour boiling water into the roasting tin to a depth of 2.5cm (1in). Bake in the oven for 30–40 minutes, until still slightly moist in the centre, but not runny.

4 Meanwhile, put the jam in a small pan with the lemon juice and 1 tbsp water. Bring to the boil, then push through a sieve. Carefully brush or spoon the sieved jam over the surface of the hot pudding.

PREPARE AHEAD The pudding needs to soak for at least 30 minutes before cooking, but can be left to soak for up to 8 hours.

serves 4

prep 15 mins, plus soaking • cook 40 mins

Chocolate puddings

A treat for all chocoholics. These simple-to-make puddings are baked briefly so that a light sponge surrounds a rich, creamy chocolate centre.

INGREDIENTS

45g (1½oz) butter, softened, plus extra for greasing
250g (9oz) dark chocolate, chopped
115g (4oz) caster sugar
4 eggs, lightly beaten
½ tsp pure vanilla extract
45g (1½oz) plain flour
pinch of salt

METHOD

1 Generously butter the sides and bottom of the moulds. Cut a piece of greaseproof paper to fit in the bottom of each and put in position, then butter. Set aside. Preheat the oven to 200°C (400°F/Gas 6).

2 Put the chocolate in a heatproof bowl set over a pan of simmering water, without letting the bowl touch the water, and stir for 5 minutes, or until the chocolate is melted and smooth. Set aside.

3 With an electric mixer, beat the butter and sugar until blended and smooth. Beat in the eggs a little at a time, beating well after each addition, then add the vanilla extract. Sift the flour and salt together, and gently stir into the egg mixture, then stir in the chocolate.

4 Divide the batter equally between the moulds: the mixture won't fill them to the tops. Put the pudding moulds on a baking tray and bake for 12–15 minutes, or until the sides are set but the centres are still soft when lightly pressed with your fingertips.

5 Put an individual serving plate upside-down on top of each pudding, then, wearing oven gloves, invert both so the pudding sits on the serving plate. Remove the lining paper. Serve the puddings hot.

serves 4

prep 10 mins • cook 20 mins

4 × 175ml (6fl oz) dariole moulds or individual pudding basins • electric mixer

GOOD WITH Softly whipped double cream or hot custard flavoured with grated orange zest.

PREPARE AHEAD Steps 1 and 2 can be prepared several hours in advance, ready for popping in the oven at the last minute.

Sticky toffee and banana pudding

A lovely winter pudding that is as fast to prepare as it is sure to be eaten.

INGREDIENTS
115g (4oz) butter
115g (4oz) light muscovado sugar
200ml (7fl oz) double cream
6 tbsp maple syrup
225g (8oz) ginger cake, sliced
2 large bananas
60g (2oz) pecan nuts, chopped

METHOD

1 Preheat the oven to 190°C (375°F/Gas 5). Place the butter, sugar, cream, and maple syrup in a small pan and heat gently, stirring constantly, until smooth.

2 Lightly grease a 20 x 30cm (8 x 12in) ovenproof dish. Arrange the cake and bananas in the dish, pour the sauce over, and scatter the pecans over the top. Bake for 10 minutes, or until the toffee sauce is bubbling.

GOOD WITH Double cream, custard, or vanilla ice cream.

PREPARE AHEAD You can assemble the pudding several hours in advance. Toss the bananas in lemon juice first and tuck them under the cake – this will stop them from going brown. Add the toffee sauce and pecans and bake just before serving.

serves 6

prep 5 mins
• cook 10 mins

20 x 30cm
(8 x 12in)
ovenproof dish

Rice pudding

A rich dish that is all the better for slow cooking.

INGREDIENTS

15g (½oz) butter, plus extra for greasing
60g (2oz) short-grain rice, such as Arborio
600ml (1 pint) full-fat milk
30g (1oz) caster sugar
pinch of ground cinnamon or grated nutmeg

METHOD

1 Lightly grease the dish with butter. Rinse the rice under cold running water, then drain well. Pour the rice and the milk into the dish and leave to rest for 30 minutes.

2 Preheat the oven to 150°C (300°F/Gas 2). Add the sugar, stir, then sprinkle the top with cinnamon or nutmeg and dot with the butter. Bake for 2–2½ hours, or until the top of the pudding is golden.

GOOD WITH A spoonful of berry jam or fruit purée.

serves 4

prep 15 mins, plus resting • cook 2–2½ hrs

900ml (1½ pint) ovenproof serving dish

Semolina

This milk pudding is warm and comforting.

INGREDIENTS

450ml (15fl oz) milk
150ml (5fl oz) double cream
115g (4oz) semolina
85g (3oz) caster sugar
3 tbsp rosewater
4 tsp jam, to serve

METHOD

1 Put the milk and cream in a saucepan and bring to the boil. Pour in the semolina in a steady stream, stirring all the time. Add the sugar. Bring to the boil and allow to simmer for 3–4 minutes. Keep stirring and, if lumps form, use a whisk to beat them.

2 Remove from the heat. If the mixture is too thick, add a little more milk. Pour in the rosewater and mix well.

3 To serve, divide the pudding between warm serving bowls. Mix the jam with 1 tbsp boiling water and drizzle over the top.

Plum crumble

A popular, quick, and easy dessert – great for family lunches.

INGREDIENTS

600g (1lb 5oz) plums, halved and stoned
maple syrup or honey, to drizzle
single cream, to serve (optional)

For the crumble

150g (5½oz) plain flour
100g (3½oz) butter, chilled and cubed
75g (2½oz) light soft brown sugar
60g (2oz) rolled oats

METHOD

1 Preheat the oven to 200°C (400°F/Gas 6). To make the crumble topping, place the flour in a large mixing bowl. Rub in the butter with your fingertips until the mixture resembles breadcrumbs. Do not make it too fine or your crumble will have a stodgy top. Stir in the sugar and the oats.

2 Place the plums in a medium ovenproof dish, drizzle the maple syrup or honey over, and top with the crumble. Bake for 30–40 minutes, or until the top is golden brown and the plum juices are bubbling. Drizzle with single cream to serve (if using).

PREPARE AHEAD The assembled dish can be frozen for up to 2 months.

serves 4

prep 10 mins
• cook 30–40 mins

freeze for up to 2 months

Bananas flambéed with Calvados

Flambéing cooks off the alcohol and intensifies flavour.

INGREDIENTS

2 oranges
4 ripe bananas
60g (2oz) unsalted butter
85g (3oz) light soft brown sugar
juice of 1 lime
3 tbsp Calvados
whipped double cream, to serve (optional)

METHOD

1 Remove the zest from half an orange with a potato peeler and chop very finely. Squeeze the juice from both oranges.

2 Peel the bananas and halve lengthways. Melt 45g ($1\frac{1}{2}$oz) of the butter in a large non-stick frying pan and fry the banana quickly until lightly coloured on both sides. Remove from the pan, cover, and keep warm.

3 Add the remaining butter to the pan and melt. Sprinkle the sugar over and heat gently, stirring occasionally. Add the lime juice and orange zest and juice to the pan. Cook over a high heat for 2–3 minutes.

4 Add the Calvados and tilt the pan towards the heat if you have a gas hob, or use a match to ignite and cook until the flames burn out. Add the bananas and turn them in the sauce to reheat gently.

5 Serve while hot with whipped double cream, if using.

Pear gratin

A sophisticated, simple, and foolproof dessert.

INGREDIENTS

4 ripe Comice pears
150g (5½oz) blackberries
60g (2oz) walnuts, roughly chopped
225g (8oz) mascarpone
30g (1oz) dark muscovado sugar

METHOD

1 Preheat the grill on its highest setting. Quarter the pears and remove the cores. Place them skin-side down into a shallow flameproof dish. Scatter over the blackberries and walnuts.

2 Drop spoonfuls of the mascarpone over the pears and sprinkle the sugar on top. Grill for 3–5 minutes, or until the mascarpone is hot and bubbling, and the sugar begins to caramelize.

GOOD WITH Crisp, buttery biscuits.

serves 4

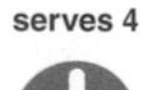

prep 10 mins
• cook 3–5 mins

shallow
flameproof dish

Kaiserschmarrn

Legend says that this Austrian pancake was created for Emperor Franz Josef. Roughly translated as "Emperor's mishmash", it is warming and delicious.

INGREDIENTS

4 eggs
100g (3½oz) plain flour
45g (1½oz) caster sugar,
  plus 4 tsp for sprinkling
150ml (5fl oz) milk
45g (1½oz) unsalted butter
45g (1½oz) raisins
icing sugar, to serve

METHOD

1 Separate the eggs and put the yolks, flour, caster sugar, and milk in a bowl. Using a balloon whisk, whisk together to form a smooth batter. In a separate, clean bowl, whisk the whites until stiff and gradually fold into the batter.

2 Melt ¼ of the butter in a non-stick frying pan. When it is foaming, pour ¼ of the batter in the pan and sprinkle ¼ of the raisins over it. Fry over a medium heat for 2–3 minutes, or until the batter is set and brown underneath, then flip over, and fry on the other side until golden brown. Set aside. Repeat to make 3 more pancakes.

3 Tear the pancakes into pieces using 2 forks. Put the pieces into a larger frying pan, sprinkle with the extra caster sugar, and cook over a medium heat for 1 minute.

4 Dust with icing sugar and serve.

GOOD WITH Plum preserve, the traditional accompaniment. You could also serve with apple preserve or fruit compôte, if you don't have plum preserve to hand.

Stewed plums

At their best in late summer to early autumn, plums are perfect for cooking.

INGREDIENTS

85g (3oz) caster sugar
1 star anise
1/2 cinnamon stick
1 orange
450g (1lb) ripe red plums, halved and stoned

METHOD

1 Place the sugar in a saucepan with 300ml (10fl oz) water, the star anise, and cinnamon. Pare the zest from the orange with a potato peeler, leaving the white pith. Squeeze the juice and add to the pan with the zest. Heat gently until the sugar has dissolved, stirring often.

2 Add the plums and gently stir to coat in the syrup. Simmer gently for 8–15 minutes, depending on the ripeness of your fruit, until tender but still holding their shape. Discard the star anise, cinnamon, and orange zest before serving.

GOOD WITH Greek yogurt and clear honey.

PREPARE AHEAD Can be made up to 2 days in advance. Keep chilled.

serves 4

prep 15 mins
• cook 20 mins

Lemon and sugar crêpes

A delicious treat for breakfast, lunch, or tea, these simple pancakes are a family favourite.

INGREDIENTS

115g (4oz) plain flour
¼ tsp salt
1 egg
300ml (10fl oz) milk
about 3 tbsp vegetable oil, for frying
lemon wedges and caster sugar, to serve

METHOD

1 Sift the flour and salt into a large bowl, and make a well in the centre. Add the egg and milk and whisk together, gradually drawing in flour from the sides, to make a smooth, thin batter. Slowly add the remaining milk, beating until smooth. Leave to stand for 10 minutes.

2 Preheat the oven to its lowest setting. Heat the crêpe pan over a high heat until hot. Pour in enough vegetable oil to coat the bottom of the pan, swirl around, then pour off the excess.

3 Ladle 3 tbsp of the batter into the centre of the pan and tilt so that it covers the base thinly. Cook the crêpe for 1–2 minutes, or until small bubbles appear. Slide a palette knife underneath and flip over, then continue cooking for 30 seconds, or until golden.

4 Remove and keep warm in the oven. Repeat until all the batter has been used.

5 Serve hot, sprinkled with lemon juice and sugar.

GOOD WITH A drizzle of maple syrup, chocolate sauce, or fruit purée instead of the lemon and sugar. These pancakes can also be enjoyed with a whole range of fillings such as stewed fruit or sliced bananas.

PREPARE AHEAD The crêpes can be made in advance, layered with greaseproof paper, and wrapped in cling film. Reheat in the oven before serving.

serves 4

prep 5 mins, plus standing • cook 10 mins

18cm (7in) crêpe pan • palette knife

freeze interleaved with greaseproof paper, for up to 3 months

Baked jam roll

This English pudding was traditionally steamed, but baking makes the crust crisper. You can use any jam, but raspberry works particularly well.

INGREDIENTS

225g (8oz) self-raising flour, plus extra for dusting
115g (4oz) shredded suet
4–6 tbsp jam
1 egg, beaten
caster sugar, to sprinkle
custard or cream, to serve

METHOD

1 Preheat the oven to 200°C (400°F/Gas 6) and line a baking tray with greaseproof paper.

2 Put the flour and suet into a mixing bowl and add 100ml (3½fl oz) water. Using a round-bladed knife, mix to a soft, but not wet, dough. Add more water if necessary.

3 Put the dough on to a floured work surface and roll to a rectangle measuring 18 x 25cm (7 x 10in). Gently warm the jam in a small pan, but do not allow it to get too hot, or it will burn.

4 Spread the pastry with jam and roll up loosely. Put on to the baking tray, seam-side down, then brush with beaten egg and sprinkle with a little caster sugar. Bake in the preheated oven for 30 minutes, or until golden brown and crisp. Serve with custard or cream.

Torrijas

In Spain, this version of French toast is usually served as an indulgent pudding rather than as a breakfast dish.

INGREDIENTS

8 slices of 1–2 day-old baguette
750ml ($1\frac{1}{4}$ pints) full-fat milk
3 tbsp caster sugar
1 cinnamon stick
200ml (7fl oz) olive oil, for frying
3 eggs, beaten
4 tbsp icing sugar, for dusting
maple syrup, for drizzling

METHOD

1 Arrange the slices of baguette in a shallow dish. Mix the milk, sugar, and cinnamon in a saucepan. Bring to the boil, stirring constantly, then pour it over the baguette slices. Discard the cinnamon, and leave the bread to stand for 15 minutes, so that it soaks up all the milk.

2 Heat the oil in a frying pan over a medium heat. Using a fork, take a slice of the bread, coat it in beaten egg, and place it in the frying pan. Repeat with a second slice, as quickly as possible. Fry the slices on both sides until golden, then repeat with the remaining slices, in batches.

3 Drain the fried slices on kitchen paper, arrange on a plate and, when slightly cooled, dust generously with icing sugar, and drizzle with maple syrup. Serve the slices while still warm.

serves 4

prep 5 mins, plus standing • cook 20 mins

Hot orange soufflés

Hot soufflés are not difficult to make, but they do need a little care. This is a basic sweet soufflé, flavoured with orange zest.

INGREDIENTS

50g (1¾oz) butter, melted
60g (2oz) caster sugar, plus extra for dusting
45g (1½oz) plain flour
300ml (10fl oz) milk
finely grated zest of 2 oranges
2 tbsp orange juice
3 eggs, separated
1 egg white

METHOD

1 Preheat the oven to 200°C (400°F/Gas 6). Put a baking tray in the oven.

2 Brush the ramekins with melted butter, then dust their insides with sugar, making sure there are no gaps.

3 Add the flour to the remaining melted butter and cook over a low heat for 1 minute. Remove from the heat and gradually add the milk. Return to the heat and bring slowly to the boil, stirring all the time. Simmer for 1–2 minutes, then remove from the heat again, and add the orange zest and juice, and all but 1 teaspoon of the sugar.

4 Add the egg yolks to the sauce, beating in well. Whisk the whites to medium peaks and beat in the remaining 1 teaspoon of sugar. Mix 1 tablespoon of egg whites into the egg yolk mixture to loosen it, then fold in the rest of the egg whites.

5 Pour the mixture into the ramekins, scraping it away from the top of each dish with a small knife. Place on the hot baking tray and bake for 12–15 minutes, or until the puddings are golden and risen, but still a little runny in the centre.

serves 4

prep 20 mins
• cook 12–15 mins

4 small ramekins

freeze, uncooked, in the ramekins for up to 1 month

Quindim

This sweet, creamy, and very rich dessert is a popular party dish in Brazil.

INGREDIENTS

100g (3½oz) caster sugar
4 egg yolks
2 tbsp grated fresh coconut
60ml (2fl oz) coconut milk
grated fresh coconut, toasted, to serve

METHOD

1 Preheat the oven to 180°C (350°F/Gas 4). Whisk the sugar and egg yolks in a bowl until light and creamy. Add the fresh coconut and coconut milk, and stir until evenly combined. Spoon into the ramekins.

2 Stand the ramekins in a roasting tin and pour in enough warm water into the tin to come halfway up the sides of the dishes.

3 Bake for 25–30 minutes, or until set. Lift the dishes out of the tin, leave to cool, and then chill for at least 3–4 hours before serving.

PREPARE AHEAD Make the quindim several hours ahead or the day before, and chill until ready to serve.

serves 4

prep 15 mins, plus chilling • cook 25–30 mins

chill for at least 3–4 hrs

4 small ramekins

INDEX

Page numbers in *italics* indicate illustrations.

DORLING KINDERSLEY WOULD LIKE TO THANK THE FOLLOWING:

Photographers
Carole Tuff, Tony Cambio, William Shaw, Stuart West, David Munns, David Murray, Adrian Heapy, Nigel Gibson, Kieran Watson, Roddy Paine, Gavin Sawyer, Ian O'Leary, Steve Baxter, Martin Brigdale, Francesco Guillamet, Jeff Kauck, William Reavell, Jon Whitaker

Picture Researcher
Emma Shepherd

Proofreader
Anna Osborn

Indexer
Susan Bosanko

Useful information

Refrigerator and freezer storage guidelines

FOOD	REFRIGERATOR	FREEZER
Raw poultry, fish, and meat (small pieces)	2–3 days	3 months
Raw minced beef and poultry	1–3 days	3 months
Cooked whole roasts or whole poultry	2–3 days	9 months
Cooked poultry pieces	2–3 days	3 months
Soups and stocks	2–3 days	3–6 months
Stews	2–3 days	3 months
Pies	2–3 days	3–6 months

Oven temperature equivalents

CELSIUS	FAHRENHEIT	GAS	DESCRIPTION
110°C	225°F	¼	Cool
130°C	250°F	½	Cool
140°C	275°F	1	Very low
150°C	300°F	2	Very low
160°C	325°F	3	Low
180°C	350°F	4	Moderate
190°C	375°F	5	Moderately hot
200°C	400°F	6	Hot
220°C	425°F	7	Hot
230°C	450°F	8	Very hot
240°C	475°F	9	Very hot

Volume equivalents

METRIC	IMPERIAL	METRIC	IMPERIAL
30ml	1fl oz	450ml	15fl oz
60ml	2fl oz	500ml	16fl oz
75ml	2½fl oz	600ml	1 pint
100ml	3½fl oz	750ml	1¼ pints
120ml	4fl oz	900ml	1½ pints
150ml	5fl oz (¼ pint)	1 litre	1¾ pints
175ml	6fl oz	1.2 litres	2 pints
200ml	7fl oz (⅓ pint)	1.4 litres	2½ pints
240ml	8fl oz	1.5 litres	2¾ pints
300ml	10fl oz (½ pint)	1.7 litres	3 pints
350ml	12fl oz	2 litres	3½ pints
400ml	14fl oz	3 litres	5¼ pints

Weight equivalents

METRIC	IMPERIAL	METRIC	IMPERIAL
15g	½oz	150g	5½oz
20g	¾oz	175g	6oz
25g	scant 1oz	200g	7oz
30g	1oz	225g	8oz
45g	1½oz	250g	9oz
50g	1¾oz	300g	10oz
60g	2oz	450g	1lb
75g	2½oz	500g	1lb 2oz
85g	3oz	675g	1½lb
100g	3½oz	900g	2lb
115g	4oz	1kg	2¼lb
125g	4½oz	1.5kg	3lb 3oz
140g	5oz	1.8kg	4lb